THE BLACK WIDOWER

The Black Widower

The Life and Crimes of a Sociopathic Killer

CHARLES LAVERY

MAINSTREAM PUBLISHING

EDINBURGH AND LONDON

First published in Great Britain in 2012 by
MAINSTREAM PUBLISHING COMPANY
(EDINBURGH) LTD
7 Albany Street
Edinburgh EH1 3UG

ISBN 9781780575315

A catalogue record for this book is available
from the British Library

Printed in Great Britain by
CPI Group (UK) Ltd, Croydon, CR0 4YY

This book is dedicated to the amazing Lavery clan.
Lang may our lums reek.

ACKNOWLEDGEMENTS

I WOULD LIKE TO THANK DEREK OGG QC, PROFESSOR DAVID Wilson, Stephen Smith, and everyone else who helped in creating this record of Webster's life and crimes. In particular, Mr Ogg's insight into the case was invaluable. Many thanks also to Dr Grieve, whose cutting-edge techniques closed this case and whose thoughts on Webster helped illuminate this effort.

CONTENTS

INTRODUCTION

FELICITY DRUMM'S MOBILE PHONE FINALLY RANG IN THE early hours of the morning at her home in Takapuna, New Zealand. The time didn't matter, she was wide awake anyway.

It was a call she had waited 12 years to take. The prosecutor on the other end of the phone, standing 12,000 miles away outside the High Court in Glasgow's Saltmarket, probably said a lot more during the call, but Felicity heard only two words: thirty years.

She thanked the caller and cut the connection, then broke the good news to her family, most of whom were gathered around.

It was her 51st birthday, and this was the best present she could have hoped for, on a birthday she wasn't supposed to see.

She had travelled to Scotland some two months previously to tell her story in court, to help convict the man who tried to kill her, the man who left her destitute, too poor to even divorce him.

She was one of three. His first victim was dead and his last had been saved by police at the eleventh hour. She, and Felicity, had been the lucky ones.

She spent seven days on a witness stand telling the story of her life with Malcolm Webster. Her loving husband. Her original statement to police was 150 pages long.

That now seemed like a lifetime ago. It had taken 12 years to see justice done, but she had never given up hope that it would be.

As Felicity was receiving the good news by telephone, her husband, Malcolm John Webster, was sitting in a holding cell underneath the High Court as guards wandered past stealing sly looks.

It was a rare sunny day for Glasgow, but architects of the city's High Court building hadn't incorporated too many windows downstairs, where the guilty were gathered.

Webster, a white, middle-class, 52-year-old nurse, was finally truly troubled. He had sat in the dock of court four throughout the longest prosecution of a single accused person in Scottish legal history, some four months in total, and had barely frowned as his crimes were revealed to an incredulous nation.

A jury had returned guilty verdicts on all counts.

He was a murderer, an attempted murderer, a poisoner, an arsonist and a thief.

In the solitude of the basement, perhaps for the first time in his life, this unlikeliest of sociopaths was forced to take stock. He had shown no emotion as the verdicts were read out, just two deep breaths before the foreman of the jury rose to announce his fate.

Webster drugged and murdered his first wife, and, having fooled police into believing it was an accident, he tried the same modus operandi years later as he attempted to dispatch his second wife, Felicity, on the other side of the world.

A third fiancée, Simone Banarjee, had been saved from his clutches by detectives who warned her that the man she loved was plotting her death even while they were planning their honeymoon.

He used drugs to stupefy his victims and fire to kill and

cleanse. At one point, he even faked cancer to elicit sympathy and gain access to their lives.

The three victims we know of all had two things in common: they were nurses and they were all independently wealthy. Police believe there may be more.

Detectives across the globe joined forces to end Malcolm Webster's Ladykiller spree in an investigation that spanned the world and took over five years.

He had torched houses, offices and cars, and was grooming a string of women as future targets.

As guards below the High Court packed his belongings into a clear bag and noted each item, the watch, the belt, the wallet and its contents, Webster baulked at only one thing: his new iPhone.

He was carrying £800 in cash in the back pocket of his trousers, and offered it to the Reliance prison guard to turn a blind eye to the phone he couldn't bear to part with. His offer was refused.

In a criminal career spanning three decades, he killed his first wife for insurance cash, tried to murder the second after taking out nine policies on her life and had just persuaded his third victim to sign over her estate to him. All it had cost Webster was a £6,000 platinum and diamond engagement ring. And someone else had paid for that too.

Almost 18 years into an audacious crime spree, he was finally caught, and sat awaiting transfer to HMP Barlinnie in Glasgow, a guilty man.

There were three dead children in a Saudi hospital where Webster once worked, a series of fires across the globe that had earned him a fortune in insurance payouts, and the hanging question: why did it take so long to snare him?

Webster had selected his clothes carefully for the trial: neutral colours, brown slacks and an open-neck checked shirt under a navy pullover topped off with an anonymous dark-blue raincoat. Over his shoulder he carried a brown leather satchel. In the morning press of commuters in Glasgow's Merchant City, he looked like any other middle-aged office worker heading for another day shuffling papers.

Bearded, overweight and sporting the now obligatory accessory of the commuter, a set of ear buds attached to his new iPhone tuned to his favourite station, Radio 4, he was an everyman.

However, as his fellow travellers bustled into offices and on to trains and buses, Webster, with presenter James Naughtie breaking that day's news through his earphones, was heading for a place thankfully few of us ever get to experience. As photographers from around the globe pinged flashes in his face each morning, he walked quietly and calmly past the phalanx into court four of the High Court of Glasgow, sat himself in the dock and watched a jury of his peers file in to decide his fate.

He had with him a copy of *The Telegraph* and his favourite glossy car magazine. By the time he had carefully chosen his anonymous outfit and sat in the dock on that first day in court, detectives had completed enough of the jigsaw to lay several capital charges against him.

Police officers don't tend to believe in coincidence. There were a great many coincidences around Malcolm Webster. The stark truth about this criminal is they may never know how many people he has killed.

Webster killed with kindness, a gentleman who sent his victims into easy fugues with drugs to ease the pain. He still claims he is an innocent man.

Today he's sitting in protective custody in jail, fully convinced that the rest of his life has been stolen from him.

Those who survived him can finally get on with theirs.

1

THE MAKING OF A MONSTER

MALCOLM JOHN WEBSTER WORKED HARD AS A CHILD, mainly at alienating those around him. Not for him the running of errands for neighbours or supplementing the pocket money from his middle-class parents. He was a loner, but a seemingly happy, normal loner of a child, content in his own company as others played football. He struggled to make real friends, but it didn't appear to trouble him greatly. Friends from that era are few and far between.

His parents were cold and aloof by all accounts, and his father in particular had some strange habits, but from the outside nobody could say that this was anything other than a happy middle-class family unit. Certainly, there were no pointers as to what lay ahead for young Malcolm.

Malcolm was born in London on Saturday, 18 April 1959, a little after twin sister Caroline. It's interesting that he should come into the world accompanied by a female, as women – in particular, forceful, independent women – would feature so strongly in his life and in his downfall.

Buddy Holly had died in a plane crash six weeks earlier and the swinging sixties were about to revolutionise the nation. However, this would have little impact on the Webster household.

His father Alexander (Sandy) was a detective chief

15

superintendent in charge of the Fraud Squad at the Metropolitan Police Service in London. Born in Kincardine, Scotland, he was from tough stock, and, by all accounts, he ran a 'Victorian' house. He was certainly a hard taskmaster who controlled the lives of those closest to him just as he ordered his highly disciplined life at work. He ruled with an iron fist. There was no velvet glove with which to wrap it.

He met wife Odette, a former nurse, when they were both working as police officers in London and Surrey. They married in East Horsley, Surrey, on 19 December 1952, and, after son Ian and then twins Malcolm and Caroline had come along, Odette gave up her career as a police officer to become a full-time housewife and mum, in what was, according to investigators, a very strange household.

Throughout his childhood, Webster, along with his mother, sister and brother, had to leave the family home in East Horsley every time their father needed to use the bathroom. 'Daddy' demanded an empty house for his daily ablutions. This was often a thrice-daily occurrence, when mum Odette would bundle them all up and take them for a walk, while Sandy Webster toileted in total privacy. This odd behaviour carried on into Webster's adult life.

At mealtimes, the children were not allowed to talk to one another, and could only speak if addressed directly by their father who, after a long day at the office, was more interested in the food in front of him than how his three children had fared at school.

Outside the home, from a very early age, Malcolm Webster seemed to distance himself from his peers, but, at the same time, would attempt to attract attention to himself with a series of bizarre random acts. These included faking medical conditions and fainting in front of school chums, classmates and teachers. They seemed to occur whenever Webster was being forced to do something he didn't want to do, according to those around him in the early years.

By the age of seven, his anti-social tendencies were so pronounced that his chums at the weekly Scout hall meetings he attended had given him the nickname 'Pyro'. From a very young age, Webster had a fascination with fire and tried to befriend other boys by impressing them with his fire-raising skills. One of his tricks, which he would use to such devastating effect in later years, involved him stealing nail varnish remover and matches and setting it on fire. It brought people closer to him, but not so close that they would be burned. His dangerous stunts, such as burning small bushes in the woods near his home or a bin packed with rubbish in the next street, may have earned him a reputation as a 'pyro', but they failed to win him many friends.

Little did the young Scouts know then that the 'Pyro' label they gave the fire-starter in their midst would ring so true in later life. It is the earliest indication of his later career of mayhem. A good nickname always seems to stick – with those who created it and sometimes even in the psyche of the person labelled by it.

As a child, Webster was thought to suffer from epilepsy and asthma and was marked out as a weakling by the boys in his local neighbourhood. He suffered from neither condition in later life, but invented all manner of ailments in an effort to attract attention. He also told people he was dyslexic in an effort to gain attention and the sympathy that came with it from the adults around him. He continued this deception into his early adult life, a relatively minor fib but one that would be blown apart decades later by a prosecutor keen to expose his liking for lies by producing samples of his well-written letters in a court of law.

The drugs he had to take as a child to combat these psychosomatic 'conditions', and rid his young body of whatever it was that truly ailed him, also marked him out as different in the eyes of other children, who shunned him on a regular basis. There was something not quite right with young Malcolm; he was the kind of boy parents warned their own children about playing with, according to some around him at that time.

However, the medical routines he went through, together with the drugs he was prescribed, would come in very handy for Webster as an adult.

The young Malcolm Webster, much like the older version, craved attention and respect but did not possess the tools to earn either. He improvised, or mimicked, the emotions he thought would bring him the attention he rarely got at home. His twin sister Caroline, a far more sensible girl, was favoured, as was big brother Ian. Webster was truly the runt in a litter of three, the lowest in the pecking order of the household, and the last in line to have his opinion aired within a strict household where 'Daddy' knew best.

Malcolm spent his days at school alone, courting friends with ever more outrageous stunts, and his nights and weekends trying to impress anybody who cared to watch with his fire-starting tricks. Nobody could really get close to young Malcolm Webster. Perhaps nobody really tried.

His family were well-heeled and aspirational, and, although they lacked the money to really make things happen for the family, he was sent to a fee-paying boys' school. He told people he had been to the elite Charterhouse, but in truth he attended a far more modest independent school.

One of Webster's oldest friends, Janet Davies, who has known him since she was 13, met him on a train on the way to school in Surrey and they both became members of an amateur dramatics society. Webster told her he had a brain tumour when he was 17 and she said he would suffer fainting fits in the drama group.

He had played both an angel and a donkey in the group's varied shows, and was never a stand-out pick for the big solo. The fainting and wild claims about his health got him the attention his poor vocals could not.

At school, he continued his deceptions and also told the

other children he had a brain tumour. He also stole money from his own home. By the age of 15 he had left school with no formal qualifications. He was frequently in trouble, but never with the police or social services. Back then, taking him to his father Sandy, the senior police officer in the Met, was probably punishment enough. There is no record of the young Malcolm being prosecuted or being brought before the courts on any matter.

After leaving school and failing miserably at a short-lived career in sales, he decided he would train as a nurse, just as his mother Odette had done prior to her joining the police service. By this time, Webster had feigned so many medical conditions he was well used to hospital corridors and nursing staff.

By the age of 17, young Malcolm Webster, the trainee nurse, had finally started making his own way in the world. His choice of career, influenced by his mother, would shape his life path in a way not even he could have imagined back then.

He also had a girlfriend. He was her first love, but she was not his.

That girl is now a married mum who declines to be identified, but she fell pregnant with Webster's child at the age of 15 and was encouraged by him to have a secret abortion. She reluctantly agreed, in an effort to save their love affair, and Webster made the arrangements. The deed was done in a back-street London clinic. Webster dumped her soon after she terminated their child.

Decades later, that first love, now a married mother herself, felt compelled to sit her aged father down and break the news of that abortion to him.

The retired businessman was shaken to the core. He said, 'I owned a nursing home at the time. I gave Malcolm a job there as he was training to be a nurse and he was my daughter's first love, first boyfriend. He wasn't a nasty boy or someone you immediately were wary of, but he always went his own way. He worked as a binman prior to me giving him the job and, when you saw him in the street doing that job, a job most young people would turn up their noses at, he seemed perfectly happy, quite content.

'It was probably because he could do it alone, didn't need to work in a team, and it was simple, I suppose.

'Soon after I employed him, things started going missing from the home. Money and trinkets. This had never, ever happened. My staff was experienced, long serving and very professional. I knew almost immediately it was him. It simply could not have been any of the rest of them.

'I sacked him, which didn't go down well with my daughter as I had no proof.

'I just knew it was him. Strangely, I got no argument from Malcolm when I called him into the office and told him he was out the door. He just seemed to take it on the chin, turned and walked out, without a single word. I thought about going to the police but really I had no proof to take to them. I was furious at what he had done, and I was glad to see the back of him. I wish now I had gone to the police, when you consider all that has happened.'

That was in 1978, at a nursing home in Bexhill, near Hastings. Webster was 19 and was finishing his training as a nurse following a stint at Epsom Hospital.

He added, 'She sat me down and told me she had something to tell me. I could see something was wrong, and then it all came out.

'She said she had just read an article about a Malcolm Webster and she told me about the secret abortion as she felt certain that the press would eventually find this information out. She wanted me to know first, ahead of any story being printed.

'I comforted her at the time but all I felt was a deep anger at the man. My daughter had been pregnant with his child, aborted it because he talked her into it and then was dumped by him.

'She then had to carry that secret for almost three decades before his actions forced her once again to relive that heartache and reveal all to me. She is happily remarried now. She has a new life. He brought that old life back to our door.'

It is believed he used the money stolen from the old folk in the nursing home to buy vinyl records and at one point a set of golf clubs. He also stole and pawned a diamond ring from one of the OAPs. It may seem like small fry, but it bore all the hallmarks of a young man who thought he could take whatever he wanted in life. He had decided to live life to his own standards, to make his own rules as he made his way in the world.

Soon after dumping this girl, the teenage Webster was seeing another girl, his first true love by all accounts. She would soon go on to kill herself. The details of that suicide are shrouded in mystery, but it was investigated by officers some decades later. They could find no proof that it was anything other than a young woman taking her own life. It was the first death of a woman connected to Malcolm Webster. Sadly, it would not be the last.

Shortly after, he embarked on an affair with a married woman eight years his senior, a nurse who had separated from her husband at that time. According to witness statements, he fell head over heels in love again. They had a passionate affair, which ended after a few months when the woman returned to her husband. Friends, in statements to police, say this devastated a relatively young Malcolm Webster. The rejection catapulted him into a downward spiral friends believe he never really came to terms with.

At this time, the young Webster decided to go travelling. He didn't stop for the best part of a decade, until a scandal in the United Arab Emirates left him no option but to return to his native England.

In fact, what has never been revealed before is that he travelled to New Zealand, Australia and to the Middle East in that decade-long period. He was away from home year after year, only popping back on brief holidays to catch up with family. He told people he had worked with Aboriginal children while in the Australian Outback, as well as working as a young nurse in schools and hospitals across Australia and New Zealand, before settling into life in the Middle East.

When he was around 30 years old, Webster worked for a time at the Tawam Children's Hospital in Abu Dhabi, in the United Arab Emirates. He left under a cloud less than six months into the job, having been the subject of an investigation into the unexplained deaths of three children. The children, all under six, died of cardiac failure in that six-month period, a very unusual cause of death in a child. What's more unusual is that Webster was on duty on each occasion and had alerted colleagues to the deaths. In fact, he discovered all three young, lifeless bodies. In the Emirates culture, the body is buried very quickly, according to custom, and there is no post mortem.

Former colleague and lover Beth Brown, who worked with him in the UAE at the time, said there had been an inquiry into Webster by health officials who suspected he may have played some part in their deaths. He was suspended from duty, according to Brown, now a 52-year-old paediatric nurse and mother-of-two, who took Webster as her lover in 1989. She also said he had acted strangely around the time of the deaths.

The three deaths were unexplained, but, as all the children were in a special-care unit at the hospital, bosses there decided there was insufficient evidence to conduct a full police inquiry. Instead, they sacked Webster just hours after the third child died.

Beth Brown said there had been 'strange incidents' on the ward. 'He left under a cloud. He was suspected of harming some of the children.

'They rarely do post-mortem examinations in the United Arab Emirates because they don't believe in them. If someone dies, it's Allah's will.'

Brown maintains that Webster was found semi-conscious after he had been experimenting with self-injection of insulin and that Abu Dhabi hospital administrators formed the suspicion that Webster had secretly injected the children with insulin too.

Rather than launch a public police investigation, the hospital security escorted Webster out of the country. Investigations have revealed that Webster's dad, the senior police officer in the Metropolitan Police, played some part in this exit from the country, and that he may have used Foreign Office staff to help in this regard. He also paid for his son's flight out of Abu Dhabi, according to investigators.

Friends say Webster's travels looked to them like he was mending a broken heart, but, by the time police officers were taking these statements, they already knew this could not be true.

A faked brain tumour at primary school, fires and the nickname Pyro, a secret abortion and control of a vulnerable woman. And all of this before the age of 20. His blueprint for later life had been drawn up.

Now, he was back in the UK, working as a nurse in Guildford, Surrey, and about to meet another woman, one who would fall head over heels in love with him. One who entrusted her life to him.

2

THE ONE FOR ME

WHEN CLAIRE MORRIS CAME INTO THE WORLD, ON BOXING
Day, 1961, the tiny, wailing bundle of joy could have no idea
that she was the Christmas present nobody wanted.

Her birth mother, a nurse at the beginning of her career, had
already decided she would give her baby away. Baby Claire had
come at the wrong time and after a liaison with the wrong man.

At the same time, Dr Charles Morris, a much loved and
well-respected GP in Kent, and his wife Betty, also a nurse,
were looking to adopt, as Betty had recently discovered she
was unable to have children.

Baby Claire very quickly became the gift Dr Morris and his
wife had prayed for, and she was adopted into their family. She
was joined 18 months later by baby brother Peter, also adopted
by Charles and Betty, intent on filling their home with the
laughter of children. For young Claire, it was to be the best of
times after such an uncertain entrance into the world.

Her early years were privileged and a young Claire was
brought up in a wealthy, loving home. Father Charles attended
to his surgery and mum Betty raised their children at their
home in Kent.

Claire quickly grew to be a leader of the pack, a bright
bundle of fun with a large circle of chums.

In 1966, her father took a position in the town of Ouyen, in Australia's Murray region, and the family emigrated there. They returned six years later, to Upchurch in Kent, when Claire was 11, and the young girl with the Aussie twang was an immediate hit with the local children, a curiosity in early 1970s England.

She was educated privately, at St Stephen's College, Broadstairs, Kent, a now defunct boarding school for 'the daughters of gentlemen'. Claire soon rose through the uniformed ranks to become a popular Head Girl. She was a slightly built girl with a good figure and wavy unruly hair she constantly moaned to friends about. She had a cheeky grin and her face lit up when she used it to full effect. She walked and talked and laughed the way a young girl without a care in the world should, according to pals. She was simply happy in her own skin.

She was not the most academic of children but made up for it with a passion for sport, in particular hockey and skiing, at which she became expert. She also developed a passion for gardening, and whiled away weekends with mum Betty in the garden of their Kent home, planting, weeding and pruning. The time they spent together only served to strengthen the bond between adoptive mother and daughter, particularly after dad Charles's untimely death when Claire was just 15, and Betty would always refer to Claire as 'my best friend'.

When the time came to leave school and venture into the world, mum Betty was the proudest parent in the world when Claire told her she wanted to become a nurse, just like she had been, and, in fact, her birth mother too.

She trained at Westminster Hospital in London and became a state registered nurse, before going on to specialise in eye care at Moorfields Eye Hospital.

It was 1991 – a happy time for young Claire, and it was about to get even better. While she was working at Moorfields, 29-year-old Claire attended a party at a friend's house. A young man across the room kept trying to catch her eye. She had never laid eyes on him before, but her heart was racing. The young man's name was Malcolm Webster.

She would tell friends that she 'knew right away' this was the man for her, his good looks, his calm assuredness, his height and clipped, well-mannered tone. She had never truly been in love before, according to brother Peter, and Webster was her one, and only, true love.

The day after the party, Webster met Claire for the second time. He was carrying chocolates and flowers for her.

After a short time, she plucked up the courage to take her true love to her parents' home for dinner. Mum Betty recalled Claire told her, 'I'm sure you'll like him. There's only one problem – he's unemployed.'

Unfortunately, Betty did not share her daughter's enthusiasm, and had some strong reservations about the 'strange' young man, although she can perhaps be forgiven for this, as Webster called her 'stupid' the very first time he ever met her, at the family dinner party.

'I didn't like Malcolm right from the start,' Betty said. 'He wasn't the sort of person I'd have married. He was strange. You don't call your girlfriend's mother stupid when you've just met her.'

However, like any loving mother, she was pleased to see her daughter happy and didn't want to spoil things by seeming not to like her new boyfriend.

At the time, Webster was looking for work around London's hospitals, and he was offered a job a short time later. There was only one problem: it was at the other end of the United Kingdom, in Aberdeen, in the far north of Scotland.

They decided they would both move there and start a life together. They both started working for NHS Grampian, and Claire began a BSc in health care science at the University of Aberdeen.

On 3 September 1993, they married, surrounded by their

families. It was a traditional affair, complete with Highland dress for the men, and they hired the splendid surroundings of King's College Chapel, Aberdeen, for the purpose. Her brother Peter stood in for their late father Charles and gave Claire away with a beaming smile and a proud heart. Her fairy-tale life with her new husband was just beginning. The future looked bright for this good-looking, happy couple.

'I was honoured,' Peter said. 'I thought she was going to have a very happy life. I was delighted for them, she seemed happy. She was in love, for the first time in her life.'

Everyone was delighted for the happy couple, despite Betty's initial reservations.

Claire, although separated from her family by almost the length of the country, had never seemed happier. The couple moved into their first new home together, a rural idyll, Easter Cattie Cottage near Oldmeldrum, Aberdeenshire, and started planning their life together. First among Claire's list of priorities was a litter of kittens. The cottage was a perfect retreat for two carers to come home to and forget the toils and tragedies of their working days, so immersed were they in the extremities of life and death.

Claire, who loved Scotland and its people, had fallen in love with a man, a job and a country. Now she was looking forward to the next chapter in their life together: babies. For now, the two kittens she had bought would do, but they were busy making plans to start a family when she concluded her studies at university.

However, family members soon began to notice subtle changes to the sister and daughter they loved so much, the girl who was so full of life.

Her brother Peter feels his sister, normally 'strong willed', quickly became more submissive to her new husband Malcolm. 'Malcolm changed Claire. My cousin Geoffrey said he was too good to be true – there had to be something wrong with him. I thought any changes in Claire stemmed from the fact she was falling in love for the first time. She was 29 or 30 years old, had never been seriously in love before, and was completely smitten.'

The young Claire Morris's life had been 'filled with laughter', according to mum Betty. The move to Scotland had taken her daughter too far away for regular, meaningful contact, and Betty found Webster 'strange' and struggled to overcome her 'instant dislike' of the man, even though Claire was clearly besotted with him.

'He just seemed odd and it's hard to put my finger on why,' Betty said. 'He didn't seem natural to me.

'Claire would call me "mum", but Malcolm didn't like that, and wanted her to call me "mother", which was something I never really got used to.

'He also used to tell her to take her hands out of her pockets and to stand up straight.'

Webster himself called his parents 'mummy' and 'daddy' right up until their deaths, and he was constantly rebuked as a child by his father for not standing up straight or for slouching around with his hands in his pockets.

Friends had never seen her so happy, albeit she regularly complained of being tired and strung out, with dry hair and a lack of energy, although, on its own, this didn't really ring any alarm bells for Claire or her friends and family, and it was put down to the move north and her body struggling to cope with the drastic change in temperature of the Northern Scottish climate.

However, friends had begun to notice how she often felt the need to sleep, sometimes through entire weekends. When they called to speak to her, Webster would tell them she was asleep and that he did not want to disturb her.

Sandra Rodwell studied nursing at Aberdeen University at the same time as Claire. She remembers Claire speaking to her about her new husband's generosity towards her. 'She said Malcolm was being very generous. It was about life insurance;

if something happened to Malcolm, then she would stand to gain and vice versa. She tended to look at Malcolm being generous to her. If anything happened to either of them, the other would be the beneficiary or something to that effect.'

It seemed, for Malcolm Webster, the honeymoon was over, and he was already putting his own plans for the future in place.

3

ANYONE ELSE IN THE CAR?

THE MAN WAS ON HIS HANDS AND KNEES IN THE WET GRASS by the side of the winding rural road, dazed and confused, crawling through the nettles, away from a crashed car.

The Daihatsu Sportrak 4X4 was down an embankment just a few feet away from a steep, sharp drop into a ravine.

Bus driver Kevin Shearer was driving along the Auchenhuive to Tarves road at Kingoodie, Aberdeenshire, on his way to collect a group of boozed-up lawyers and their partners from nearby Haddo House Hotel when he turned the corner and came upon the accident, just before midnight. The headlights of the crashed jeep were still shining brightly into the woods beyond.

'I saw a person on all fours on the verge,' Mr Shearer said. 'I did not see anyone else. The person was crawling towards me, but didn't do anything to attract my attention.'

He ran to the man crawling along the verge to ask if he was OK. The man, seemingly uninjured, said something about swerving to avoid a motorcyclist. Mr Shearer immediately asked if anyone else was in the car. Malcolm Webster, the man on his hands and knees, told him no.

An experienced rural driver, Mr Shearer then searched the immediate area for the biker Webster had mentioned, fearing

31

he too could have come off his motorbike and was lying hurt somewhere in the dark undergrowth. Having found nothing, he returned to the crashed jeep and looked inside.

He later told police, 'I looked into and under the jeep, a Daihatsu. I could see the floor pedals on the driver's side, but could not see any other person inside.'

Mr Shearer ran to a local farm to alert them and ask them to call the police. While he was gone, a small fire started in the engine compartment of the crashed jeep, and began to take hold.

Shortly afterwards, Elizabeth Smith drove past the scene of the accident en route to collect her boyfriend from a night out. She spotted the jeep with its headlights on and assumed someone was 'lamping' for foxes, using headlights to spot the creatures in the woods. She did not stop, as it was dark and she did not see anyone by the car.

Ten minutes later, on her return journey, she saw a man lying in the verge with a woman kneeling over him. She and the boyfriend she had just picked up pulled over. Ms Smith got out of her car and walked towards the crashed jeep, where she saw Webster's wife Claire Morris lying unconscious in the reclined passenger seat as the engine compartment of the vehicle began to burn more fiercely.

As she increased her pace towards the prone lifeless figure of Claire Morris, evidently knocked out by the impact of the crash, the car burst into flames.

'I can remember bits of it like it was yesterday,' she said. 'It was horrific when I saw the jeep in flames and the woman lying in the seat. If I had stopped the first time, I would have been able to pull her out. I remember me saying, "Was there anyone with you?" He didn't answer. He closed his eyes. I asked him again if there was anyone with him because he had opened his eyes again.

'I remember asking him again. I remember him saying his wife. I shouted that his wife was with him and, just as I was shouting that, the jeep blew up.

'The door burst open and she was lying with her seat reclined and her leg fell out of the car.'

Elizabeth Smith watched as Claire Morris was consumed by the flames, unable to go to her aid. The image has tormented her since.

Ms Smith's original statement from 1994 describes how she saw smoke pouring from the bonnet of the car before it burst into flames. It also states that there was no movement by Claire Morris to escape the vehicle, not even when it began to burn.

Other witnesses spoke of seeing Claire's body lit up by flames in the interior. Eyewitnesses also later recalled seeing melted petrol cans behind the driver's seat. The fire could be seen from two miles away, and, distressingly, Claire had to be identified by her dental records, so fierce was the fire that claimed her life.

By the time the car burst into flames, Webster had told three people who arrived at the scene, including an off-duty police officer, that there was nobody inside the 4X4.

He had been dazed, confused and concussed, and remembered Claire was inside the jeep only seconds before it blew up in a fireball. By then, it was too late for anyone to help her.

Malcolm Webster and his new bride Claire had been married just eight months.

Earlier that night, at home in Tarves, Webster had been working on a report for Aberdeen Children's Hospital that had to be on the manager's desk for 9 a.m. the following day. It was 11.30 p.m. on 27 May 1994.

Webster decided to drive to Aberdeen that night to deliver the report. Claire said she would go along for the ride, according to police reports from the time.

Webster loaded the car with water and a sleeping blanket, as he said his new wife would often fall asleep during car journeys. They set off just before midnight. Halfway along the road, Webster said he had forgotten something from home and turned back, but, instead of taking the same route back home, he took a more rural road. Coming upon a bend in the road, in the dark, he had been dazzled by the headlight of a motorbike approaching them fast on the wrong side of the road.

Webster swerved to avoid the biker and lost control. The jeep ploughed off the road and down a steep embankment, before hitting a tree and coming to rest.

He gave a police statement at the time of the accident, as he lay in hospital recovering, grieving the death of his wife. He said, 'The first thing I remember is getting out my door. I had to use my leg to push it open.

'I think I saw trees outside her door and I decided I couldn't get it open. I knew I could not kick it open from my side. I decided to pull Claire out my door.

'I'm sure I said something to her and I recall her screaming. A scream I have never heard before.'

He claimed that, if the motorcyclist had stopped, they could have got Claire out of the car.

'I couldn't get her out. I remember smelling smoke and petrol and another smell I can only describe as warmth. I remember crawling through stinging nettles up to the road.'

After the crash that had just killed his young wife, Webster was given oxygen at the scene and later examined at Aberdeen Royal Infirmary, around 4 a.m. on 28 May 1994. His pulse and blood pressure were absolutely normal just a few hours after the accident, although Webster was complaining of pain. Dr John Hiscox, 48, a consultant in emergency medicine at Aberdeen Royal Infirmary, said the 35 year old's heart rate was a steady 72 beats per minute.

Webster stayed in ward 50 of the hospital for seven days and planned Claire's funeral from his sickbed. He selected a passage from Shakespeare's *The Merchant of Venice* for her headstone: 'For she is wise, if I can judge of her. And fair she is if that mine eyes be true. And true she is, as she hath proved herself, and therefore, like herself, wise, fair and true, shall she be placed in my constant soul.' A battery of tests, including a CT scan, was carried out during those seven days and doctors could find nothing to explain the symptoms of which he complained. Webster told police officers he had fractured ribs and a neck injury, as well as aching muscles.

Mum Odette and dad Sandy became his constant companions. Odette clucked about her son's bedside and struggled to grasp the reality of the horror that had blighted Malcolm's life.

Meanwhile, in Kent, Claire Morris's mother Betty, dressed in her finery to attend a family wedding in Kent, had opened her front door to two grim-faced uniformed police officers.

The looks on their faces told Betty everything she needed to know. She knew right away, as most mothers uncannily do, why they were there. 'It's not Claire, is it? She's not dead, is she?'

They were words to steal a sliver of the soul of any officer given the gruelling task of breaking such news.

When one of the officers confirmed that was the reason for their visit, Betty simply replied, 'She's my best friend,' before inviting the officers in, offering them tea and showing them pictures of her beloved daughter.

She also told the officers that her daughter Claire had called her just the day before to tell her about a near-miss she and Malcolm had had, while driving a month earlier, again on a remote road in the Highlands. Webster had taken Claire out on a long drive into the country and they had gone off the road. Only a small bush saved them going over a ravine, Claire told her mother, and a local farmer had apparently used his tractor to pull them out of the ditch.

Betty added, 'This one didn't result in any injuries but it was a nasty one as the car rolled. She said a bush had stopped the car going down the hill. Claire said Malcolm was very tired.'

In the weeks leading up to the fatal crash, Claire Morris had told friends she felt unwell. She had no idea why. In fact, on 26

May 1994, the day before she died, she had been to a keep-fit class in Tarves with pal Lesley Roberts, and as they chatted afterwards, she told her, 'I'm not right, there's definitely something wrong with me.'

Claire told her she would make another appointment with her doctor, having already been there complaining of fatigue.

Lesley, who lived near the Websters in Tarves, was also a nurse and actually worked with Webster. She had become good friends with Claire in the six months before her death.

Just two days later, on Saturday, 28 May 1994, Joanna Reid, an NHS manager working at Aberdeen Royal Infirmary, called to tell Lesley that Claire had died. Lesley agreed to go to Claire's home to collect clothes for Webster, who was still in hospital after the crash.

As she sorted clothes out at the cottage, she spotted three bottles of hospital medication on the coffee table. 'I saw a box of Epilim. I knew it was an epilepsy drug.'

She said she also saw a bottle of Carbamazepine, another epilepsy drug, and another bottle which she could not identify. All of the bottles were, she claimed, issued by Aberdeen Royal Infirmary.

Neither Claire nor Webster suffered from epilepsy.

4

UNTRULY, MADLY, DEEPLY

AS THE TAUT CORDS RESTRAINING THE OAK COFFIN WERE released slowly through the hands of the pallbearers, Claire Morris's family embraced tightly as they huddled together and watched her body descend. It was their last chance to say goodbye.

The grieving husband, Malcolm Webster, wore a white medical neck brace, stark against the black of his mourning suit, and a horrible reminder to them all of what had brought them together on this bleakest of days at Tarves Cemetery in Aberdeenshire.

Claire was a popular girl and it was a busy graveside. Webster, tears in his eyes, was being supported on one side by his dead wife's brother Peter. He clasped Webster's hand with his free left hand as a coffin cord ran slowly through his right. On the other side of the grieving husband was Claire's heartbroken mum Betty, also taking time to comfort the big broken Englishman who had swept her daughter off her feet.

Webster was sobbing loudly and could be seen physically shaking at the graveside, wracked by the overwhelming emotion of the day and the scene before him; his beautiful young bride of just eight months was being lowered into the ground before his eyes. It seemed too much for him to bear.

Betty squeezed his hand tightly in a loving gesture, even though he had been unable to save Claire, her 'best friend', in the crash. Webster was the man who had been behind the wheel on that fateful night, the man whose driving had caused the death of his wife. He was beside himself and, while Claire's mother Betty was angry with him, she tried to console him in his grief.

As they held hands over the windswept open grave in Aberdeenshire, they were all there to say their final goodbyes to a young woman they had loved with all their hearts. They tried to take comfort and support from one another. A grieving husband, a loving brother and a broken mother.

Indeed, Peter Morris would later recall that the day they said goodbye to Claire at the cemetery in Tarves Webster was 'crying, apparently heartbroken. I was squeezing his hand in sympathy. I thought we were grieving together. He'd lost his wife; I'd lost my sister.'

Seemingly so overcome with emotion was he that Webster left the cemetery before some of the mourners could pay their last respects or offer him their sympathies. He wanted to get away from this desolate scene.

Claire was just 32 when she burned to death, trapped inside the family car. She had been married to Malcolm Webster for just 32 weeks.

It appeared to have been a tragic accident.

There were, however, some friends at the time who questioned this. They raised concerns but these were dismissed by the authorities.

Claire's best friend, nurse Lesley Roberts, was united with mum Betty over Webster from the beginning. She didn't like him either. She also believed he was cheating on Claire and was convinced her best friend's death was not an accident.

'Immediately after the crash I went to their cottage to pick up some of Malcolm's things to take to him at the hospital,' she said. 'There I saw epilepsy drugs on the table. Neither

Claire nor Malcolm had epilepsy. I was suspicious then. I knew something wasn't right.

'At the funeral, Malcolm sobbed and seemed upset but I couldn't shake the feeling he'd had a hand in her death.'

Lesley took her fears to police in Aberdeen but they were dismissed. She says she had nightmares about Claire's death for years and feels that perhaps there was more she could have done at the time.

There wasn't, not after the police force that investigated the accident dismissed it as just that. No foul play, case closed.

A forensic examiner concluded that the fire had started in the engine compartment shortly after the impact with the tree and that this had caused the death of Claire, as her husband lay concussed and dazed some distance from the vehicle, unable to communicate effectively with would-be rescuers.

In 1994, Sandra Rodwell, who was studying with Claire and lived near the Websters, visited Claire on the morning of the crash. 'She was fine, but anxious and was concerned about Malcolm. He was tired and was working hard.'

After the funeral, Webster visited Sandra and, apart from a neck collar, she said he seemed uninjured. Webster told her he had been blinded by a motorcyclist and went off the road.

'He said he walked round the car to check if Claire was all right. I'm sure he said she acknowledged that she was OK. It wasn't a complete story. I was going to ask questions, when he said he heard Claire screaming when he was away from the car and it was on fire and that shut me up.'

Her husband John Rodwell was also concerned by the fact that Webster had crashed on a rural road he should not have been on. He feels there was a more direct route to Aberdeen than the one taken by Mr Webster on the night of the crash, a more direct, more open and safer route.

Former nurse Sarah Dawidek said she and her husband both sent letters to the procurator fiscal following Claire's death. She said Claire told her about a car crash she and

Webster had been involved in before the one that claimed her life. Claire had told her that Webster was driving and she was a passenger when their car had gone off the road and into a ditch.

She would often call Claire at home between 8 p.m. and 9 p.m. only to be told by Webster that Claire was already fast asleep.

'She would say she was always tired and cold,' Sarah recalled. 'She would say it was Scotland. She wasn't used to the cold temperature, but it was a concern for her.'

Several eyewitnesses, including police officers and firefighters who attended the scene, raised concerns at the time over whether this was just an accident.

One officer, traffic cop David Allan, 55, was a sergeant in the Grampian force at the time. Two of his officers, Ian Wallace and Ronald McLaren, had come to him with concerns over the 'accident' and he took their fears to senior officers within Grampian Police.

Mr Allan said the traffic officers who had raised their concerns were 'of the highest professionalism and integrity'.

He contacted a uniform inspector and CID on their behalf at the time. 'I think I phoned the CID inspector to try to get some CID involvement in the case,' he said. 'I received a call from a superior officer saying they had looked at this and they now had to draw a line under it. A decision had been made that the thing was going no further at that time.'

Ian Murray from Grampian Police – now an inspector – had just 22 months' police service when he got the call to attend at the crash site that night. He said, 'It was sometime after midnight; we arrived in a police vehicle with blue lights.'

He saw a car on fire and a man lying in the road. 'There was already the duty sergeant and inspector and two members of the public there.'

Mr Murray and Ian Wallace – now 46, and a chief inspector – were concerned about the version of events supplied by

Webster. So concerned was Wallace, in fact, that he revisited the scene several times.

At that time, Wallace was a constable in the traffic department in Aberdeen and had examined Webster's Daihatsu Sportrak after the accident.

'I mulled it over for some time. I was unhappy with the circumstances,' he said. 'I returned to the scene with my colleague Ronald McLaren to see if we could determine what had happened.

'I also returned to the scene when off-duty such was my unease with what I had seen.'

Mr Wallace spoke to an inspector about his concerns and also to his supervisor in the traffic department. He said he had found a melted petrol can behind the driver's seat in the car.

His colleague Ronald McLaren – now a chief superintendent – shared those concerns. He said, 'It was quite a significant step at that time to raise it with senior officers in that manner.'

William Rout, a group manager with Grampian Fire and Rescue Service, was also called out to the crash. He too said something 'wasn't quite right' with it.

All of these professional misgivings were dismissed.

In the months leading up to her death, Webster and Claire had taken out a dozen life insurance policies worth tens of thousands of pounds.

Webster went on to submit a claim less than two weeks after the fatal crash.

He had bought the policy from neighbour Jamie Tunstall, who had been a guest at their wedding.

Mr Tunstall spoke briefly to Webster at the funeral of his wife. 'I recall he had a neck brace, he had his arm in a sling. He was kind of shuffling as he walked.'

The last time they spoke, Mr Webster was driving around in a new car. Webster had bought a replacement, a Land Rover

Discovery, and a yacht. Claire's death had made him a relatively wealthy man.

One £53,000 policy payout was designed to pay off the mortgage. It never did.

The insurance policies, totalling £208,000, were paid out in June 1994. He was also awarded a widower's pension. By that November, virtually every penny had gone.

Webster was also quickly seeking solace in the arms of another woman, Patricia Malcolm.

Patricia had written to Webster, with whom she worked at Aberdeen Royal Infirmary, after Claire's death. She wanted to 'let him know I was there for him as a friend'.

Webster quickly invited her over for dinner. After dinner, Webster put on the romantic comedy *Truly Madly Deeply*, one of Claire's favourite films. In that movie the main protagonist is bereaved, but is watched over by her late partner as a ghost.

Patricia recalled, 'He lay across me while we were watching the film with his head on my knee. I felt a little bit uncomfortable but I didn't know what to say or do. I just sat there.'

She said that, at the end of the film, the dead partner moved on, saying it was about how 'the partner should move on and live her life the way she wanted to'.

They also went for dinner at a local hotel restaurant, with Webster collecting Patricia in his new Land Rover 4X4. He even told her he 'wanted to come and take me out in his new car'.

That trip involved three hours of driving but Webster showed no signs of fear or distress, in the wake of the crash that killed his wife. In fact, he seemed happy to talk to Patricia about the accident.

'He was outside the car,' she said. 'I think he said he had been knocked out, and when he came to he heard Claire screaming and the car was on fire.'

Webster also took Patricia to Claire's graveside.

In fact, in the years immediately following Claire's death, he seemed somewhat obsessed with taking women to the cemetery in Tarves, Aberdeenshire.

Brenda Grant, from Kansas City, Missouri, of whom more later, was also taken there. Webster had befriended her by email, and she travelled to Scotland to meet him.

Brenda first met Webster in August 1995, just over a year after Claire's death, and by that autumn she was in an intimate relationship with him.

She said he spoke with her about the accident. 'I understand it was a car crash and she didn't survive. I thought he had possibly fallen asleep. His feet were burned from it. I didn't probe a lot. He would get very emotional. I recall him saying he'd fallen asleep at the wheel. He got extremely emotional any time he talked about Claire.'

Catherine Brown, yet another former lover, was also taken to Claire's grave, when she visited Webster in Ballater, Aberdeenshire, and they spent the weekend in a hotel together.

Webster told her his last recollection of the crash in which his wife died was her screams.

In December 1994, after a string of relationships, some failed, and some ongoing, Webster secured a job with an IT company selling specialist medical software to hospitals in Saudi Arabia, and once again left the UK. He told friends the memories of Claire and of the accident were too painful and a clean break might help.

He settled into a new life in Saudi Arabia, and, at a dinner party one fateful night in Riyadh, in May 1996, he found himself sitting next to the woman who would become his second wife.

5

AN ENGLISH GENTLEMAN

FELICITY DRUMM WAS IN ALL SENSES OF THE PHRASE A self-made woman. Sitting at the dinner table in a friend's Riyadh home, she was taken by the way the big Englishman next to her, with his clipped BBC Radio tones, talked about his parents, quaintly labelling them 'mummy' and 'daddy'.

She liked him, he made her laugh. The evening was going well and for once she had reason to thank her friends for inviting someone along for her. Some of their previous choices had been the subject of frank exchanges after the cheese and biscuits.

Nurse Felicity was alone at the dinner table on that evening for a reason; she had spent a large part of her life working hard to make her future more secure. It was why she was in Riyadh in the first place. That, a broken heart and a mortgage that needed paying.

She had not found the time to look for a partner, so her friends had been doing the job for her. And, for once, it seemed they had come up trumps. Working ten-hour shifts at the local King Fahd Hospital did not leave a lot of time for socialising, but at least, by 1996, Felicity had managed to pay off that mortgage back home in Auckland, New Zealand, and was building up a nice nest egg in her bank account, tax-free of course.

45

This solid work ethic had been instilled in her by her father Brian, a Takapuna high school principal. She had been brought up in a loving, happy family home where she learned that hard work brought its own rewards.

Now here she was, reaping those rewards, enjoying a dinner party, listening to Malcolm Webster, a handsome 30-something, regale her with tales of travelling the world. He had even visited her home nation, and, Felicity thought, shared her passion for seeing the world.

Felicity grew up a happy girl in Auckland surrounded by loving sisters Jane and Katherine. Her parents, Edward Brian and Margaret, ran a happy home. Her dad, known as Brian, was head teacher at the local secondary school. Felicity, therefore, really had no choice other than to be a well-behaved star pupil, but she was popular among her friends, despite her father's often stern role in their upbringings. After graduating from school, she decided she would become a nurse.

She duly qualified and began to work as a nurse in Auckland, New Zealand. There was only one problem; she was tired of working three jobs just to pay her bills. She had a NZ$100,000 mortgage to pay off, and she longed for a better life.

After a chance conversation with an old friend, she decided to move to Saudi to be able to earn tax free, and pay off her debts. She got there through character, hard work and determination.

Working ten-hour days at the King Fahd Hospital in Riyadh as an oncology nurse was tough, but it had been worth it. She had earned enough to pay off her mortgage and the money she had borrowed towards it from her parents, as well as saving up a nest egg of NZ$98,000 in the bank.

Now she had met Malcolm Webster at that dinner party and they had fallen in love. Felicity was happy. Life was finally going her way.

Felicity said she was instantly attracted to Webster, although in the beginning he pushed their relationship harder than she did. The Kiwi cancer nurse found him funny, witty and entertaining. 'He spoke like a BBC announcer and I found him a bit twee because he referred to his parents as "mummy" and "daddy", which I found hilarious.

'He asked me out the following week to dinner and that's when we started seeing more of each other.'

Webster's middle-class jovial computer-geek image seemed to earn the trust, then the affection of women around him. He wasn't a sexual predator, he was an English gentleman.

Within a few months of meeting Webster, Felicity had opened her heart to him on her reasons for being in Riyadh. She told him she was mortgage-free back home in New Zealand and had money in the bank, thanks to the pay rates and the long work hours.

By January 1997, just eight months after meeting her at that dinner party, Webster had proposed to Felicity on a holiday trip to the UK. The eight months preceding the proposal had been bliss, with chocolates, flowers and the love of a kind, caring man, and Felicity agreed without hesitation.

They returned to New Zealand and married in St Andrew's Catholic church in Milford on Auckland's North Shore, on 26 April 1997. The family threw a huge party, and Felicity's sister Jane's husband was Malcolm's best man and her children already called him 'Uncle Malcolm'.

Webster impressed his new in-laws, Brian and Margaret, with his open, affable character. Jane was especially impressed after Malcolm called to ask her advice on whether Felicity would like diamond and sapphire earrings as her 'something blue' on their wedding day. 'Who wouldn't?' was Jane's immediate reply.

The happy couple honeymooned at Cooks Beach on the Coromandel Peninsula, but, on the first night of their new life together, something strange happened.

Felicity, who had packed fish and lamb chops to take to the remote beach idyll for the first two nights' meals, made dinner for them, then, after drinking a cup of tea, she slept for a solid 36 hours. When she finally came to, she was shocked. Nothing like that had ever happened before; she was a fit, healthy woman.

'I challenged him, when I couldn't believe he had left me sleeping for 36 hours,' Felicity recalled.

'But he got out of it by saying I'd woken up and gone back to bed but obviously couldn't remember. He even said he had fed me.

'He was my closest friend; I would have no reason to be suspicious of him at all.'

Felicity had felt so unwell after the coma-like sleep that she sought medical help. The sleeping and symptoms of fatigue continued long after they returned from their idyllic honeymoon.

Sometimes, nurses can be the worst type of people for sorting their own ailments, but Felicity was worried enough about the fatigue to get checked out. Dr Jonathan Simcock, a neurologist with 45 years' experience, examined Felicity after she complained of blackouts, headaches, double vision and fatigue.

She also told the doctor there was an acrid, bitter taste to everything she ate.

Dr Simcock, 73, initially diagnosed a vertebral migraine. He had wanted to reassure Felicity that she did not have epilepsy or a brain tumour, her two main fears.

Around this time, the couple decided to relocate to Scotland, where Webster had found employment in Aberdeen. However, two days before the couple left New Zealand, Felicity received some disturbing news from her GP, Dr Julie Hancock, after she went for a blood test. The results showed a problem with Felicity's liver, with her symptoms displaying the same characteristics as those for victims of date-rape drugs. While, of course, this was very worrying for Felicity, the hassles and logistics of moving abroad forced her concerns to the bottom of her list of priorities.

The couple flew to Scotland in May 1997, and moved into

Easter Letter Cottage at Lyne of Skene, Aberdeenshire, for Webster to begin his new job.

A few months after they arrived in the north-east of Scotland, Felicity broke the news to Webster that she was pregnant with their first child. She naturally expected tears of joy. Instead, she saw another side to her new husband.

Webster reacted in fury. He charted all the reasons they should not have a child, how much babies cost to raise being top of the list. Felicity says he did eventually calm down and even began to look forward to the birth.

Throughout this time, she was sleeping for long periods, slurring her words and losing her balance. She became so concerned that there might be a risk to the health of her unborn son that she went to the doctor when she was 16 weeks pregnant. No conclusion could be reached and it was put down to the stress of the move and the pregnancy.

In September 1997, Felicity had her first glimpse of Webster's fascination with fire, when she lost everything she owned in an unexplained fire at their Lyne of Skene cottage in rural Aberdeenshire.

She arrived home to find the cottage partly gutted by fire. Webster was already there, and he said he had come home in the nick of time. He told her not to worry as they were insured. He also said he had managed to save some things. Felicity never received an explanation for the fire.

Her handbag, containing her New Zealand driving licence and other identification documents, was never seen again.

Several months later, Felicity spotted her driver's licence propped up on her husband's desk in his study, but, assuming he had simply forgotten to mention that he had managed to recover some items after all, she thought little more about it.

With the birth of their son Edward in May 1998, the couple decided they would move back to New Zealand, so that Felicity could be closer to her family and the support that she would inevitably need in the coming years.

In preparation for the move, they put all their belongings in storage at the huge Shore Porters Society facility in Aberdeen, a long-established and respected Scottish moving firm. Their distinctive red-banded retro removal vans are a common sight on the roads of Scotland and beyond. The firm was founded in 1498, six years after Columbus discovered America. The joke goes they helped move Noah to the ark.

On 12 November 1998, the massive storage facility at the company site, housing the beloved possessions of literally hundreds of families, including Webster and Felicity's worldly goods, was set alight.

The fire raged for days and over 80 firefighters attended the scene. The final cost of the blaze and the destroyed goods within its compound would exceed £5 million.

A detailed investigation into the cause of the fire concluded that workmen repairing a section of the roof had somehow left a hot gas blowtorch on the roof which had ignited.

It transpired that Webster had been there moments before the blaze took hold, to retrieve some vital paperwork from his storage space.

He had been sitting with Felicity and friends visiting for the evening in their Lyne of Skene cottage, watching an episode of *London's Burning*, the drama series about firefighters, when he announced that he was heading out to buy some recordable CDs from a computer shop next door to the Shore Porters facility. He told Felicity he would pop into Shore Porters while he was there to pick up some paperwork for his brother Ian. Both men were keen genealogists and Webster had researched his family's roots back to the 14th century. He had a suitcase in storage which contained all the data of their family tree. As he was emigrating to New Zealand, he thought it wise to leave the documents with the family in England.

He drove to the storage facility and returned home some time later. Webster, Felicity and their friends then watched events unfold on TV as news broke of the massive blaze. TV crews broadcast live on the night.

As they watched, Felicity realised the place storing everything they owned was burning before their very eyes.

Felicity recalled, 'When the warehouse burned down we lost everything – all I had to my name was a single suitcase. It was a horrendous time.'

But Malcolm had calmly told her, 'It's all insured. It's only things.'

He then told the group of his good fortune, that he had been there earlier that day and retrieved the family-tree data from the facility. He walked out of the living room and returned with the case he had collected.

When he opened it, all present discovered it contained nothing but Felicity's underwear. He had picked up the wrong case.

Owners of the Shore Porters Society have always denied their workers caused the fire. Nobody has ever been convicted of starting the 1998 fire and it was not treated as suspicious at the time.

One week after the blaze, Webster filed an insurance claim to the firm for £87,847. CGU Insurance disputed the amount and Webster was even quoted in the local newspaper complaining about the delay in paying out his claim. They eventually settled the claim and paid Webster £68,000. Shortly afterwards, the couple left for New Zealand. Webster had refused to leave Scotland before the insurance claim was settled.

When they finally returned to Auckland in late 1998, they stayed with Felicity's parents, Brian and Margaret, while they finalised the purchase of a new dream home they had set their hearts on in Takapuna, close to the rest of Felicity's family. By this time, like many married couples, Webster and Felicity had pooled their resources. He was to sell his cottage in Aberdeenshire and contribute the proceeds to the new house.

She had also allowed her new husband access to her bank account and would put up the other half of the cost of the house. She also sold her own mortgage-free home to give them a bigger pot, and therefore a chance of a bigger new home.

Webster told her he was having real problems having his share for the new house transferred from Scotland. This dragged on into early 1999, until it was getting perilously close to Felicity losing the huge deposit she had put down on the house.

Then, in February 1999, disaster struck. There had been an arson attack at the home they planned to buy, the six-bedroom villa in North Shore, Auckland, where Felicity longed to bring up their son. She had already staked NZ$60,000 on it by way of a deposit. Someone had pushed papers through the letterbox and set light to them.

A few days later, with just one week left to sign the papers on the new home, and with no sign of her husband's money arriving from Scotland, they were roused from their slumber at her parents' home by yet another fire. Webster, who had been in the bathroom a short time earlier, was awoken by Felicity after she heard a loud crack. He told her to go back to sleep. She insisted he check out the noise. Eventually, he got up and, on seeing the blaze, raised the alarm.

An armchair was on fire in an upstairs living room. Felicity grabbed baby Edward from his cot and fled outside the family home, while her dad Brian ran up and downstairs with buckets of water and Webster filled a kettle from the toilet to help extinguish the flames.

The property was not destroyed, but it was damaged badly enough for everyone to have to move out to Felicity's sister Jane's house.

As they were tackling the blaze, Webster told a stunned Brian Drumm, 'We'll laugh about this later.'

Felicity was shocked by this series of horrific events, and she realised they could easily have died in the inferno, but at this time she was also sleeping for long periods and still struggling with her health.

A week after this latest fire, 12 February 1999, was the final deadline for signing the paperwork on the new house. Felicity and Webster got into her Honda Accord to drive to the bank and her lawyer's office in Auckland. After everything they had been through, and with all the setbacks, it was a huge relief.

In the absence of Malcolm's money appearing from Scotland, Felicity's dad had put up some of his life savings and persuaded a lawyer friend to help with the rest. Malcolm assured them it would be only a matter of weeks before their investment would be repaid, when the 'archaic' Scottish banking system finally got round to wiring Malcolm's share.

As they drove over the Auckland Harbour Bridge to the bank on that fateful day, Webster began to complain that the car steering was 'wonky' and that he was having trouble steering the car.

As they reached the North-Western motorway, Webster was shouting at Felicity that the car was out of control and it began weaving across the lanes of motorway traffic. It was also picking up speed.

She said, 'He started weaving across all the lanes. We were travelling at high speed and he was weaving across lanes.

'The car went across to the right across two lanes of traffic, then back across another two lanes of traffic.

'We were travelling at high speed towards a motorway lamp which was going to hit my side of the car. I was screaming at Malcolm to watch out for the lamp. I grabbed the steering wheel and turned it towards Malcolm. There wasn't anything wrong with the steering, the car responded.'

Webster had already stopped the car twice on the journey to the bank and said he thought there was something wrong with the steering.

The car ended up in a ditch, but there was only minor damage and neither Felicity nor Webster was injured. Webster got out immediately and shouted at Felicity to stay inside the Honda. She had other ideas.

Felicity recalled, 'He jumped out and was screaming at me to stay in the car and that it was too dangerous to get out. Malcolm opened the boot, but there was no way I was staying in a ditch.'

When Felicity insisted on carrying on to the bank and to the lawyer's office to sort out the finance for the house they planned to buy, Webster clutched his chest and claimed he was having a heart attack. A police officer who arrived on the scene called an ambulance for Webster.

'He clutched his chest again, went all clammy, said he was in pain, and got all tearful,' Felicity said. 'He said, "I love you, Felicity," and said he had left me well provided for if anything happened to him.'

He begged her to go with him to hospital, and, even though she knew they were risking losing their dream home and an awful lot of money, she realised she had to go. 'I would have struggled if he had died and I was off at the bank,' she explained.

Traffic policeman Anthony Wood, 45, was one of the first officers to arrive at the scene, shortly after reports of a car leaving the road came through his radio. Webster told him that he had been travelling at 90 kph when the vehicle veered to the left uncontrollably, went down a bank and hit a tree.

Mr Wood noticed that there was only very slight damage to the Honda Accord, which Webster had been driving, and wrote him a ticket for careless driving.

Felicity was beginning to unravel, and could not believe the run of bad luck that had followed them since their happy courtship in Saudi Arabia.

However, a week later, on 18 February, their fortunes seemed to change. Malcolm announced that the money he had been waiting on from Scotland had finally arrived, and they could now press ahead with their plans to buy the villa of their dreams. He also told Felicity to get their son dressed, as he was taking them all for a picnic to celebrate and had found a lovely spot a short drive away.

Felicity could not have been happier and set about putting together a family picnic. As she drove to the designated picnic spot, with Webster giving directions beside her, they argued playfully over the best way to get there. Webster handed her a water bottle 'to keep your fluids up'.

That's the last thing Felicity can remember of that day, until the incessant ringing of a mobile telephone roused her from yet another deep slumber.

She recalled, 'It was three in the afternoon. I was slumped in the passenger seat of our car, struggling to open my eyes and didn't have a clue how I had got there. I could hear the mobile phone ringing, that's what woke me up.

'The last I could remember was driving Malcolm and our baby boy for a picnic near our home.

'We had been waiting months to buy our dream new home because Malcolm said there had been problems in getting money transferred from his account in Scotland where we had lived before.

'But that day he said the cash had arrived and we would celebrate the start of a new life with a picnic on the coast, about an hour from Auckland.

'Malcolm said he'd found this forest nearby with a lovely lake to sit for a picnic. It was a really hot day and he gave me some water to drink as I drove, following his directions. It was the last I remember before the phone started ringing.

'As I struggled to push myself up in the car I realised I was in a remote forest, almost dark because the pine trees stretched up to the sky all around. Everything was blurry but I could see Malcolm pushing our son in his buggy about 300 yards away down a rough track.

'I answered the mobile and it was my dad, sounding very anxious. "Felicity, you have to come home right now. It doesn't matter what Malcolm says, you just have to stop whatever you're doing and get home. It's serious."

'I knew something was very wrong so I clambered out the car and shouted to Malcolm to come back.

'He had a complete meltdown. "What the hell are you doing awake?" he shouted. "You need to get back to sleep. I was just going for a walk."

'He didn't want to go back home but I said I thought something really bad had happened to someone in the family and we should drive back immediately. On the way back to my sister's house, Malcolm was really sweating and was very agitated.

'As we pulled into the driveway, he turned and said, "Your dad's going to tell you a lot of nonsense about me and your money."

'The moment we stopped, Malcolm left me and our son in the car and walked off.

'My parents arrived. My father sat me down and said, "Felicity, all your money is gone."

'At that moment, I knew my husband had been trying to kill me, and that he had killed his first wife.'

6

MARRIED TO A MURDERER

THE TELEPHONE CALL BRIAN DRUMM MADE THAT DAY undoubtedly saved his daughter's life.

As he roused her from her slumber in a dark forest, he had no idea he was ruining a well-constructed murder plot. He also had no idea he had just saved his daughter from a fiery death.

When Felicity got home to her father's house, she was horrified to find the boot of the car filled with petrol, wood and newspapers. She believes the man she loved was pushing their son away to safety before returning to the car to set it alight. This realisation buckled her knees. She also realised that she had been drugged that day, and probably from the first day of their honeymoon, if not before.

'He was administering drugs to me from the start, even when I was pregnant. At 16 weeks, I had tests done because I thought there could be something seriously wrong with my baby.

'At the time, Malcolm was being very tearful. Now I'm thinking that was him realising he shouldn't have done that to an unborn child.'

Baby Edward had always suffered badly from eczema. It cleared up a matter of weeks after his father walked out of his life. Hair samples sent for testing also confirmed the prolonged presence of drugs in Felicity's system. The news was another hammer blow.

It's easy to read about a series of fires, long unexplained sleeps and car crashes and think that the woman at the centre of all of that must have been pretty stupid not to realise what was happening to her. But love is a strange drug, and many have succumbed to its powers. That, combined with the eminently plausible, unflappable Malcolm Webster, and it's a little easier to see how blinded one could be.

Felicity Drumm is a strong, clever woman, from a strong, clever family and, in the fullness of time, Webster would discover this to his cost.

Felicity had some strong allies to rely on – her family, especially her father Brian. She says she owes her dad her life. Suspicious about his daughter's constant blackouts and poor health, Brian began looking into her new husband, especially after he was faced with risking his life savings on the promise of money from Webster.

What the former high school principal eventually found, and the timing of his call to his daughter, was the difference between life and death.

Brian gently laid out the findings of his secret probe into Webster. Felicity, her world reduced to cold hard facts relayed by her father in the living room of her sister's home, could barely breathe. Webster had even begun to plan his escape.

'I opened Malcolm's laptop and saw emails to estate agents back in Devon and Cornwall saying he was moving back with his infant son and was interested in several properties,' she said.

That wasn't all. There were return flight tickets from Auckland to the UK for him and young Edward. One person was missing. The wife he had planned to kill.

Even more chillingly, prosecutors would later discover that, when Webster booked the original flight tickets to New Zealand, he bought returns for him and his son and a single ticket for Felicity.

Felicity and her father then returned to her parents' house, where she and Malcolm had been living, to search for more evidence. By now, fear was the predominant emotion. Anger had not yet kicked in. Felicity and her dad thought they were in a race against time, and perhaps even Webster, to get to the home and secure any evidence against him that they could then take to the police.

For all they knew he was already there, or on his way. Felicity now knew in her heart that her husband had murdered his first wife, and she cried as her father sped home.

Felicity and her dad searched their home and what they found there was staggering. They had beaten Webster to it and they found a briefcase containing no less than *nine* insurance documents, bearing Felicity's signature, documents that she had never signed. Her mind immediately flashed back to the driving licence propped up on Malcolm's desk, the one seemingly lost in the flames at their Aberdeen home. Had he been practising forging her signature?

The life insurance policies, with her forged signature, valued her life at NZ$1.9 million, around £940,000.

The documents fell through her fingers and at times it was too painful to focus on them. Here was his deception laid bare, in ink, on crisp company letter-headed paper. Her dad hugged her as they attempted to piece it all together. He knew one thing above all else, his daughter had been a very lucky girl.

'As soon as I saw all the life insurance policies at my parents' home, when Dad showed them to me, I knew instantly then that he had murdered Claire,' Felicity revealed. 'I was absolutely gutted. I couldn't . . . imagine how anyone could do this to somebody else who had done nothing but love and care for them. And, you know, I had a child with this man.'

Her elder sister Jane joined them and immediately realised Felicity's signature had been forged. 'I looked at her name and signature and knew it was forged,' she explained. 'Her handwriting is quite distinctive and it hasn't changed since we were at school. As soon as I saw that, I knew he was intending to kill her.

'All the trauma in our family in that incredibly short period of time; the fire, the money and house problems, the crash. It was all explained.'

Felicity also looked through her husband's computer emails. There were notes telling friends Felicity was suffering from post-natal depression after the birth of their son. There were messages to former colleagues claiming she needed close supervision for her own safety. With a cold shiver, she realised he had been preparing the ground, and possibly laying a trail for his defence should anything go awry with his heinous plan.

She also found that the cold, calculating Webster had bought a number of antiques in New Zealand using their joint account and had arranged to have them shipped back to the UK. As she would come to discover, Malcolm Webster just couldn't help himself with other people's money.

All this, and the can of petrol hidden in the boot of the car. This was the man whose first wife had died in a car blaze. A man who had vowed never to carry fuel in his vehicle again.

There could be no doubt.

'The full horror hit me. My husband was trying to kill me. That moment in the forest was meant to be my last.

'My dad had saved my life. If he hadn't phoned the mobile when he did, I'm pretty sure Malcolm's plan was to push our baby away to safety and burn me in the car as I was drugged unconscious.

'My dad knew our lawyer and bank manager and had done his own investigations. He'd been suspicious of Malcolm and he'd been proved right.'

By now, Felicity also realised Webster had planned to kill her a week earlier, on the road to the bank. He knew his ransacking of her life-savings would have been exposed had they got there. It would later emerge that the boot of the Honda was also stuffed with petrol cans and newspapers. As Webster had screamed at Felicity to stay in the car, he was at the back, with the boot open, trying to light the fire that would kill her and save his skin.

It had taken the intervening week for her dad to acquire the necessary proof to present to his daughter. Had his detective work taken just one more day to complete, he would have been organising his daughter's funeral.

Almost every penny she had, over £200,000, was now resting in Malcolm Webster's Clydesdale Bank account in Aberdeen, Scotland.

Felicity realised she had nothing left. Her bank account now showed a balance of just NZ$12. She hadn't been receiving statements, as Webster had secretly rerouted them to a post office box after taking control of the monthly finances.

By this time, Webster had booked into a motel room in Auckland. Felicity, struggling to process the vast array of information she now had on this monster she had married, arranged to meet him the next day to confront him. She needed answers. She met him in the car park of the motel as her uncle sat nearby, affording her the protection she had never got from her husband.

She told Webster she knew what he had planned for her.

Chillingly, he replied, 'I gave you a son and a good life – you'd have died happy.'

These were the last words she got from a man to whom she had given her life, whose son she had borne. Her world was in tatters. Those made of lesser stuff might have completely crumbled at this point. Felicity Drumm headed straight to her local police station.

As she sat with detectives, outlining her story to them in what would become a seven-hour statement session, her husband Malcolm was heading for the airport. He had overstayed his welcome in New Zealand, and was about to do what he was very good at, walk away from the wreckage and on to pastures new. He never looked back.

Detectives at Takapuna Police Station listened to Felicity's story. She told them about Claire's death in Scotland in 1994, the fire in their Aberdeenshire cottage, the storage facility fire, which netted Webster a £68,000 insurance payout, and fires at the house she wanted to buy in New Zealand and at her parents' home.

She described how they had met, how he had driven off the road with a boot full of petrol cans, how he had drugged her and driven her into the forest. How he had wiped out their bank account behind her back.

For New Zealand Police Service detective Glenn Gray, it was the first day of a very long 'job'. He didn't know then, as he took notes and asked Felicity to slow down, that it would be 12 years before he would see a conclusion to this macabre tale, in a courtroom on the other side of the world.

Gray acted quickly, but it was already too late to catch Malcolm Webster. He was gone. International warrants were issued for Webster's arrest just hours after his father Sandy, the former senior Metropolitan Police officer, had spoken with his son and organised his swift return to the UK, via Australia. His father also paid for the ticket.

Gray made enquiries with Grampian Police, outlined his fears and sounded officers out about the Claire Morris death crash. He was told it had been an accident, and the Grampian force refused to reopen a case they considered closed, regardless of what had happened in New Zealand. It was on the other side of the world, and nothing to do with them.

Felicity and her family were deeply frustrated by this lack of action on the part of the authorities, but it is true to say that most police officers groan inwardly whenever a cross-jurisdictional case comes across their desk.

She never gave up, however, and nor did Glenn Gray. Together, they worked away at the case, and Gray became a family friend. A nurse with a weird and wonderful story and a small-town detective, who, having checked what he could, believed her and, more importantly, believed in her right to justice. Both of them also wanted to make sure Malcolm Webster could not kill again.

It would prove to be a very long road, but Felicity Drumm was made of stern stuff.

She was going back in time on a horrible journey, remembering everything Webster had told her about the 'accident' that had claimed his first wife's life, about that first meeting in Riyadh, her episodes of ill health which, she realised, dated as far back as when her relationship with him first began. She also had to face the fact that he had risked the life of their unborn child by repeatedly doping her. This, above everything else, drove her on.

Felicity had to piece together her memories in a completely perverse way. She had to rearrange seemingly happy memories into the shards and splinters of her new reality, what she now knew to be true.

She thought back to the fires, at their Aberdeen home, at the Shore Porters storage facility, at the home they wanted to buy and at the home of her parents. How could she have been so naïve? She thought of the car crash and the wonky steering that worked when she tugged on the wheel.

She thought of waking in the forest, of sleeping for 36 hours on the first night of her honeymoon, of the frequent visits to the doctor complaining of fatigue. Her worry for her unborn son and the realisation that, even after he was born and she was breast-feeding Edward, she was passing on the poison that Webster had given her.

Webster had relocated to Auckland, New Zealand with Felicity and their baby son in November 1998. Records show that he was given a six-month visitor's visa on 15 November 1998. Former New Zealand immigration manager Michael Loulanting explained that travellers granted these kinds of visitor visas, mainly backpackers, would be required to have a return ticket before they would be allowed into the country.

He added that any non-New Zealand resident intending to settle there would have to apply to the New Zealand High Commission before travelling to the country.

Webster, given his good character, skill as an enrolled nurse and his New Zealand-born wife, would have been 'successful' at that time, had he gone through those channels. Of course, it was now clear that he had no intention of staying in New Zealand after Felicity was dead.

Webster was later barred from New Zealand. A border alert was flagged on his immigration number. This would flash up when his passport was swiped upon arrival. It was made active in May 1999, shortly after he fled the country, as Felicity told her tale of woe to concerned detectives.

The standard international alert warns airport immigration officials if someone is not allowed to enter their country and also lets them know if any agencies within that country need to speak to the person attempting to gain entry.

Webster did indeed try to return to New Zealand, on 19 August 1999, but records show he was refused entry, even though warrants were in place for his arrest by that time. Cops in charge of the New Zealand investigation were alerted at that time. Webster was there for the taking, but they felt they did not have enough evidence to take him to court. They were, however, determined not to allow him into the country because of the potential risk he posed to Felicity, the one living witness at any future trial. They were also busy trying to persuade Scottish authorities to reinvestigate the death of first wife Claire at that time, to no avail.

Webster told border officials he wanted to stay for a month to settle affairs with his now estranged wife and sort out custody and visiting rights over their child.

Officials, acting on advice from the police, refused to grant him entry and he flew on to Sydney, Australia, instead.

Detective Glenn Gray was worried Webster was coming back to finish what he had started, and leave no witnesses.

It was the only time the records showed him trying to return to New Zealand, although Webster told a string of people he had visited his son there. This was untrue, a lie spun by him to cover the fact that he was a wanted man on the other side of the world and that a police probe had been launched against him.

Gray liaised with Interpol, Strathclyde Police and Grampian Police over the case, which would eventually also involve the Federal Bureau of Investigation in the United States.

The Auckland officer also commissioned an expert report on the fire that had broken out at Felicity's parents' house when she and Webster were staying there.

The dogged officer followed a trail of evidence about Webster's alleged frauds and fire-raisings. That trail took almost a year to bottom out, and included witness statements from the Drumm family, a cache of bank statements, life insurance documents and bank transfer letters unearthed by Felicity from among Webster's belongings, along with two petrol canisters which were also found by her dad.

'It took us the best part of three months just to work through what Felicity told us, just to confirm everything that she had told us,' Gray said. 'The sheer telling of the outline of it took hours and we had to stop her and take notes. It was a big story to work through.

'For example, she didn't have first-hand knowledge of what had happened to Claire Morris in Scotland; she only had what Malcolm had told her to go on, so we had to go and check that what she had heard was true. But at that early stage we knew that, if everything she had told us stacked up, we were dealing with a murderer.

'There were ups and downs with the case, mainly caused by the cross-jurisdictional nature of it. After a year, we had taken it as far as we could take it and we put in place some immigration measures for Felicity's safety, in case he returned to New Zealand.

'I spoke with Webster briefly at the beginning of the case. When you looked at something in isolation, he could explain it away, but, when you looked at the whole range of things he was involved in, it went beyond mere coincidence.

'Everything that we had laid out showed that he was planning to kill Felicity for his own financial gain.'

Shocked detectives gathered evidence that he had robbed her life savings, drugged her with powerful sedatives to such an extent that she would sometimes sleep for 36 hours straight, even while pregnant with his child, and tried to burn down two homes. He had also tried to kill his wife in a staged car crash.

While he was targeting her, Felicity's sisters spoke of Webster telling them he feared for Felicity's sanity.

'He told me he was greatly concerned about Felicity's mental health,' Katherine Drumm recalled. 'He said it was his belief she was suffering some sort of profound depression. I was very worried to hear that.'

Jane Drumm said Felicity had told her she sometimes wondered if her new husband was slowly poisoning her. She said she was shocked to hear her sister say such a thing at that time and added, 'I said to her, "Felicity, you can't think something like that or your marriage is over."'

The Drumms rallied round Felicity and each played their part in unravelling the macabre tale.

It was Jane, who would go on to play a crucial role in the story, who found a petrol can in her sister's car. 'It made me feel shocked when I saw that. They weren't going across the Gobi desert. I couldn't understand why someone whose wife had died in a car accident would have a petrol can in the car.'

And Felicity's brother-in-law, David Pointon, decided to investigate following the car crash where Webster had tried and failed to torch their Honda car as Felicity struggled to clamber free from the passenger seat.

On 12 February 1999, he visited the pound where their damaged Honda Accord had been taken. David found a petrol can in the boot and a disposable plastic cigarette lighter in the centre console between the front seats.

The lighter being there was unusual as neither Webster nor Felicity smoked, and David added, 'It seemed a strange thing to have in a concealed yet convenient space.'

Felicity speaks of the 'Oscar-winning performance' after the car crash in Auckland that convinced her Webster was having a heart attack. He even began to cry.

The level of deception involved in robbing and trying to kill Felicity Drumm speaks of a man who is an accomplished fraudster and criminal. Detectives on both sides of the globe believe he got away with it for so long because he was following a well-rehearsed script, his own MO for murder.

Her father Brian, 82, said, 'Nothing like this has happened in our family. Nothing like this has ever happened in very many families. It took a long while to come to terms with it. But we have, we have risen above it.'

Brian said Webster was 'pleasant, courteous and smiling' when he first met him, but said the 'scales fell from my eyes' when he made the shocking discovery that his beloved daughter's bank account had been plundered.

Brian also found an antique wooden walking stick and scrunched-up newspapers crammed into a recess in the car boot, beside and all around the spare wheel.

Felicity's mother Margaret, 80, believes Malcolm Webster walking into their lives 'destroyed our innocence. It has affected us in so many ways. It has ruined our happy retirement, something we could have expected. As a family, it has been something that has brought us closer together. It's been unreal. It's like something that was happening to someone else and we were just watching from the side-lines.'

New Zealand detective Glenn Gray investigating Felicity's claims also visited her doctor and suggested she had been given a sedative from the Benzodiazepine group, such as Librium, Valium or Rivotril.

The doctor said this theory 'totally changed my outlook' on her symptoms. 'It became very clear to me that everything she had told me fitted with this.'

And it seemed that not every member of the Drumm family had been taken in by the charms of this most cruel deceiver. 'Something didn't sit right,' recalled Felicity's uncle Denis, an Auckland accountant.

Another uncle, Peter Drumm, added, 'He was a real bloody conman, let's face it. Felicity's no mug. She's got her head screwed on the right way and as far as I could make out this was the real thing for her.'

Felicity added, 'On a whim, he could put me to sleep. Hindsight is a wonderful thing when it's all laid out in front of you and you obviously look at things in a different light. It actually says something nice about me that he targeted me. I don't look for the bad in someone, I look for the good.

'I was gullible, but he was very convincing. He was very skilled at what he did. Even when he was drugging me, not once did it enter my head that he was responsible.'

Incredibly, Webster sent Felicity a letter after fleeing New Zealand when he realised the game was up. It reads like a love letter: 'I still regard you as the most important person in my life. You are the person I want to spend the rest of my life with. We can get through this. I'm either an optimist or a fool, but I just want to tell you I love you.'

Perhaps most distressingly for Felicity, she found herself in the unenviable position of battling to keep custody of her own son, while at the same time trying to get his father locked up for attempting to murder her.

After he fled from New Zealand, Webster spent years trying to gain access to his son through the New Zealand court system. His father Sandy funded this long legal battle.

As the custody battle raged, all Felicity could say was that her estranged husband was the subject of a police probe. To be more specific before any proper investigation had begun would be to tempt fate.

Webster, on the other hand, used the allegations as a basis for stating his wife was not a fit and proper person to be caring for their son.

Felicity added, 'Even Malcolm's dad told me they would make sure that he got custody of our son and claim I was unfit to care for him. The family put me through years of court proceedings and never faced up to the reality of what he'd done.

'He picked the wrong family . . . he made a mistake taking on the Drumms.'

In a macabre aside, Felicity's sister Katherine bought a camcorder from Felicity who was cash-strapped after Webster cleaned out her bank account in New Zealand and went back to the UK. When Katherine got the camera home, she found some film on the memory card, showing the Drumm family during happier times, at a barbecue with Webster behind the lens shooting the film.

'It appeared to be like a little film,' she said. 'This was my family on a joyous day but the music appeared to be quite sad and mournful. It was the type of music that might be played at someone's funeral.'

Nobody had any idea how the music came to be overlaid on the happy family shot; it had certainly not been playing at the time the video was shot.

Was it Webster's private idea of a sick joke to himself? Did he know that the scene he was filming, that of a happy family at ease in one another's company, was about to be shattered by his actions?

Perhaps viewing such a happy family scene served to remind him of everything he didn't have as a child. The funereal music, from the movie *Titanic*, was perhaps laid over the images as his own personal joke, because he believed that at some point in the very near future this happy family would be grieving for a loving daughter, killed in a tragic car accident, consumed by the flames.

Arrest warrants were issued for Webster in 2000. He faced four charges, two fire-raisings, an attempted murder of his wife and the stupefying of Felicity with drugs. But Webster was nowhere to be found.

In 2003, he did send a series of letters, from a remote post office box on the west coast of Scotland, to his son and to Felicity. They were strange and rambling letters, described in more detail later in this book.

In the letters, Webster accused Felicity of making 'wild and untrue' allegations that he drugged her repeatedly and tried to kill her in the 1999 car crash.

He also wrote to his son Edward, and spoke of fishing and computer consoles.

After the letters, the trail went cold, and could have stayed that way had it not been for Jane Drumm and a chance encounter with a senior British police officer several years later. In recognition of her work on domestic violence, Jane was awarded a Winston Churchill Fellowship in 2006 to work with Leeds Police to see how domestic violence cases were handled in the UK.

She was staying with a female police superintendent, 'a very kind, remarkable woman who looked like Helen Mirren, but younger and even prettier', and Jane told her about the Webster saga. When she mentioned that she planned to drive to Oban and confront him, the senior officer talked her out of it, for her own safety. What Jane Drumm had told her concerned the officer so much she made preliminary calls that very evening.

Jane was interviewed by Scottish detectives, who travelled south to meet her for the purpose. She had planted the seeds for a new inquiry that would cost millions of pounds and span the globe as police officers gradually began to realise the sheer scale of offences.

The hunt for Malcolm Webster had begun. And Felicity Drumm had her sister to thank for it.

Although, to the Drumm family, everything seemed to go quiet again, and they began to fear that Webster would never be brought to justice, the wheels had been set in motion. A preliminary search of the electoral roll by UK police turned up an address for Malcolm John Webster.

He was living in Oban, on the picture-postcard west coast of Scotland, with Simone Banarjee, a woman of independent means, and he was engaged to be married for a third time, despite still being married to Felicity, who had steadfastly refused to divorce him in the hope that this would prevent him finding another victim before police could catch up.

Simone was an attractive nursing manager and Webster's net was already closing around her. Detectives realised they would have to act quickly to close their net around Malcolm Webster first.

7

A FINAL ENGAGEMENT

THE POLICE OFFICERS HAD BEEN IN POSITION SINCE THE day before. They were in plain clothes, and they were edgy. The woman they had been sent to protect was not playing ball, and they had been well briefed on how dangerous their target was.

She was in shock, of course, and had little knowledge of the very real danger she was in.

Two senior detectives had walked into her office 24 hours earlier and handed her an Osman letter warning her that her life was in peril.

Osman letters are usually given to gangland figures or career criminals, for whom it's a part of everyday life. They are named after teenager Ahmet Osman, who was shot and wounded in 1988 by a man obsessed with him. It later transpired that police were aware of the threats against Osman and judges ordered a tightening up of intelligence protocols, which led to the invention of the warning letter.

A few witnesses in high-profile prosecutions had received them in the past, but none of the officers working on this case had any experience of something like this.

Simone Banarjee, a theatre manager, engaged to be married and trying for a baby with the man of her dreams, had to sit down in her office and read a letter from police stating they believed her life was at risk, at the hands of the man she had just agreed to marry. A man, police discovered, who was feigning cancer and who had just become the sole beneficiary of Simone's entire estate. Malcolm Webster had been a busy boy.

She had not acted on the information on the day the officers warned her, but they had asked her to alert them ahead of any confrontation. They wanted to be there, in numbers, at that time. Just in case.

Now officers were in position to move in quickly to the home she shared with her husband-to-be, should he react violently. Some senior officers may even have been hoping that he would. It would give them the hard evidence they needed to put this man away, rather than rely on a court case based on circumstantial evidence.

Detectives were at the front and back of the house and posted in the street. Some were positioned less than ten feet away from the kitchen where Simone would confront the man she had agreed to marry, who was now a stranger.

They had to get this right. They had to protect this woman. Her life meant nothing to him, and everything to the strangers surrounding her home.

It was the endgame of an operation that had spanned continents, taken years to pull together and had led police to fear for Simone Banarjee's safety. By this time, Webster was well along the road in his plan to kill her for her money.

Simone recalled that fateful day when her whole world came crashing down. 'It was a normal day, I was at work when two CID officers from Strathclyde Police arrived at the hospital and asked to see me privately.

'We went into the manager's office and they read the letter to me then gave me it to read and keep.'

The letter had been signed by the assistant chief constable. 'It mentioned his date of birth, Felicity, the charges outstanding in New Zealand and that my life was at risk if I continued in a relationship with him.'

This was the man she was engaged to marry, the man with whom she had embarked on a course of IVF in order to start a family. Simone realised in that instant she knew nothing about him, or of his past. But she could not bring herself to believe it.

'My initial reaction was disbelief,' she admitted. 'I thought it must be a dreadful mistake. Surely, he's not married. The person I loved was kind and caring, this was ludicrous rubbish.

'I put the letter in my desk drawer; I didn't know what to do. I went home that night feeling quite detached. It takes time for your brain to comprehend that kind of information. The police had told me to inform them if I was going to discuss anything with him that night. I didn't. I wanted to figure out what to do. To see if there was any possibility I could see Malcolm as this person.'

The next day, as officers waited outside, she returned home and found Webster in the kitchen. She confronted him with the words: 'I think there's something we need to discuss, namely Felicity. And I can probably give you your engagement ring back.'

This attractive and intelligent woman with deep-brown eyes was clever enough to come out fighting, and it had the desired effect. It put Webster on the back foot, but Simone suddenly realised the danger she was in.

'As soon as I said the police had told me, there was a complete change, almost like the shutters coming down, like the mask slipped. He went white and very quiet. It's the scariest situation I was ever in.

'I realised from my nursing training dealing with difficult patients that I had left myself no escape route from the kitchen. There was a police officer outside, but it might have been too late for that.

'I was completely at Malcolm's mercy. If I could have snapped my fingers and disappeared into the floor I would have. I dared not move. This wasn't my Malcolm. It lasted about five seconds and then he went completely back to his old self.'

Malcolm Webster had been cornered, in a place he felt safe, a place he felt he had made his own, through his usual manipulation and mind games. His face was white with anger, not red with shame, in the certain knowledge that the police had penetrated his fortress of deceit.

In fact, once he quickly regained his composure, Webster walked silently past Simone and went upstairs, where he spent a short time packing a bag before leaving the home they shared, without another word. He took time to print off just one document, in which he gave up his claim to her estate, handed it to her and calmly walked out of her life.

Officers tailed him out of the sleepy west coast town of Oban for half an hour before they were called back to guard Simone's house. It had been a long, strange day.

Simone met Webster in August 2004, on her first day at work at the Lorn & Islands District General Hospital in Oban, where he was working as a nurse specialising in the manual handling of patients. Both of them earned around £28,000 per annum.

Simone, an attractive 41-year-old, who had recently been promoted to an NHS theatre manager, was of independent means and financially secure, thanks to a trust fund set up by her parents, dad Subhash, a 79-year-old former consultant oral surgeon at the Cumberland Infirmary, and mum Elizabeth, 73, herself a former nurse.

An only child, Simone grew up in Carlisle and attended Stanwix Primary and Trinity schools. She was an excellent pupil, well behaved if a little introverted, according to old pals. She had a small circle of friends she still sees to this day.

Happy and successful in her career, Simone was ready to complete her life by getting married and starting a family. Webster would prey on this maternal instinct.

A FINAL ENGAGEMENT

When they met for the first time at the hospital, Simone was busy faxing her dad the details of a £270,000 house she was interested in buying, seeking his advice. Webster looked at the paperwork for the house and said it looked good. He claimed he had once been an estate agent. Another lie.

As they carried on chatting, Simone told him she would be buying the property outright, and mentioned the trust fund her parents had set up for her. Webster smiled approvingly, his calculating mind no doubt working overtime.

Simone Banarjee could have had no idea of the deadly consequences of this friendly chat with a new work colleague: she was now in the sights of a man devoid of feelings who wanted to take her life and everything she valued.

At that time, Webster was involved with another woman, but quickly ended it no doubt seeing a bigger prize in Simone. She sensed his attraction to her and ended a relationship she was in, although it would be over a year before they finally got together in late 2005. Both of them were studying for a master's degree in healthcare law at Salford University.

She described Webster at that time as a 'well-spoken gentleman who treats you well. He was a John Lewis man. There were no big, massive gestures, just a constant drip of nice things.'

Initially, he didn't want to talk to Simone about his first wife Claire, and described himself as a widower. When he did open up, he would become tearful when speaking about the accident that had befallen his first love.

He also took Simone to visit Claire's grave, as he had many other women.

Police believe a murderer will always return to the scene of his crime. For Webster, that scene appears to be the final resting place of his first wife. Was he drawn there to gloat at his skill in not being caught, and felt a special thrill by taking his next target with him, using his sob story as a lever to prise open the door to their hearts? We will probably never know.

When he did talk about Claire's death, the version of events that he gave Simone was far from the truth. He told her that he could not get Claire out of the car and that he had also been trapped for a time inside the burning vehicle, burning the soles of his feet before he managed to crawl out. He tearfully relived the scene as they stood at Claire's graveside in Tarves and said he could still hear his wife screaming.

'I was told he was in intensive care for about a week after the accident. He didn't like things on the television where there were screams and fires because it reminded him of the accident.'

This was the man who rated *London's Burning* as among his favourite TV dramas.

Chillingly, he also told Simone that Claire had been pregnant when she died. This was untrue, but police believe Webster said it to hook Simone further into the IVF course they had embarked on together. At that time, she was also blissfully unaware that he already had a son in New Zealand.

Webster could not have known, despite his cunning, that the different stories he told to so many people would be stitched back together by a dogged team of investigators intent on painting a true picture of the man. Claiming that Claire had been pregnant when she died naturally caused huge upset in the Morris family, but, for the manipulative Webster, it was just a means to an end.

Just before Christmas 2005, a few weeks after they got together, Webster delivered a bombshell. He told Simone he was terminally ill with cancer.

Simone says he called her on the day he buried his dad, Alexander, to break the tragic news. 'He told me the Royal Marsden Hospital in London had confirmed it was chronic lymphatic leukaemia,' she recalled. 'I felt there was no one who was so unlucky in the world to have people die on them and then be diagnosed with a terminal disease. We became romantically involved not because of the tragedies, but in spite of them.'

At this time, Webster was renting a cottage 20 miles away from Simone's four-bedroom cottage overlooking Kerrera in Oban Bay, but he had set his mind on moving in with her. He put his acting skills to good use and often called her in the middle of the night, supposedly in agony from the cancer eating at his body, and Simone would drive straight over to comfort him. One night, Webster complained of headaches and fatigue and rang her in the middle of the night to tell her he was 'very sore and scared'. When Simone arrived, 'the pain had gone and he was a bit more settled'.

At that point, Simone realised she could not leave him on his own.

'He was so caring, so attentive; he would open the car door for me, make sure that perhaps dinner was ready when I came home from work. You couldn't have wished for a better person. A real charmer would sum him up very well. But he seemed an honest kind of guy as well. My moral compass wouldn't let me run out on somebody that was suffering such an illness.'

In January 2006, the month Webster started his 'treatment', she asked him to move in with her. His master plan had worked. Simone conceded his poor health meant their relationship had moved faster than it would have normally. 'There is no way he would have come to stay here if he had not been ill or receiving treatment.'

Simone travelled to Luton to meet Webster after his first course of 'treatment' at the Royal Marsden. 'The picture of him with his head and eyebrows shaved was the sight that greeted me at the airport. I was shocked but tried to put on a brave face.'

She would be horrified to discover that, in fact, he had shaved his own head, eyebrows and body hair just to complete his ruse. In fact, so thorough was his deception that he would even lose weight and puncture his own arms with needle marks.

In the following months, Webster would also claim he was receiving treatment in Glasgow and Aberdeen.

In February 2006, Simone changed her will to leave her estate, including a £50,000 shares portfolio, to Webster. He told her he had done the same, although she never saw any proof of this.

Although no evidence was found that he had set up life insurance policies on Simone, Webster stood to gain more than £300,000 in the event of Simone's death.

At home, he suffered from what Simone dubbed the '10.30 syndrome'. 'It would happen around 10.30 p.m. and he would go into a state of semi-collapse. He could not get up the stairs without assistance and would suddenly become very tired.'

Strangely, he never took time off work for his treatment, preferring instead to use up holidays and days off in lieu. It is only with hindsight that Simone, and investigators, realised this was because Webster would not have been able to produce the necessary doctor's note.

When a worried Simone dropped him at the airport for his chemotherapy appointments, little did she know that Webster was actually seeing other women. He even flew to Paris with old flame Brenda Grant for a week-long holiday. He told Brenda he was divorced, and he also lied to her that he had cancer.

In fact, Webster cheated on Simone with at least three other women, and they're only the ones police hot on his trail could find.

In September 2006, Webster asked Simone to marry him over dinner at a local hotel, and produced a £6,000 diamond and platinum ring. Felicity Drumm, the woman he was still married to, had paid for it, albeit unknowingly. Her stolen life savings had been put to good use by Webster, a small investment towards his future.

However, that ring and his proposal of marriage would come back to haunt him.

In late 2006, Webster's condition appeared to have stabilised and the couple went on a dream holiday to Sydney and Perth, in Australia.

'At the time, I thought it was great that he was fit enough to go,' Simone recalled. 'It was the holiday of a lifetime with the man I loved.'

She could have had no idea how wrong she was.

At the same time as Simone was planning her wedding, a global investigation into her husband-to-be had gathered pace, and it would be Webster's murderous honeymoon plans that would finally bring Strathclyde Police to her door.

Simone and Webster co-owned a 38 ft yacht, *Nina*, which was moored at Oban, and were planning to spend their honeymoon participating in the ARC (the Atlantic Rally for Cruisers), a transatlantic race from the Canaries to the Caribbean.

Strathclyde Police had been probing Webster's background since receiving a tip-off from Grampian Police about his past, and when they learned he was living with a woman 'of independent means', alarm bells rang loud and clear.

Detective Inspector Charles Henry, now retired, was a key detective central to the police case, and he was convinced Simone was 'in absolute danger'. In the spring of 2007, he received information that the couple might be planning to do the ARC on their honeymoon, and was certain Webster planned to kill Simone.

'It is a transatlantic race from the Canary Islands to the Caribbean and would take about three or four weeks. We looked into it and the boat was capable of such a trip. A major fear was that that was going to present the ideal situation for him,' he explained. 'Simone was in absolute danger and I was convinced she was going to be his next victim.'

Police believed that he planned to throw her overboard at sea and claim her fortune. It would be very difficult to prove it had been anything other than an accident.

Detectives visited Craobh Haven Marina, near Lochgilphead, where the boat was kept, and put a harbour master on alert to report any activity around *Nina*.

Mr Henry said, 'We told the harbour master it was imperative if there were any preparations he knew of to let us know straight away.'

They also briefed human resources staff at the hospital where they both worked to report any holidays the pair booked, but with no hard evidence there was little else they could do.

'We were extremely concerned but I felt our hands were tied. We knew about this individual in the community who had probably murdered his first wife, had a good go at murdering his second wife and seemed intent on fleecing women that he met of their life savings.

'Almost immediately, we had been trying to get a disclosure to tell Simone about his background but we were refused because we didn't have anything new and Webster's crimes lay outside our jurisdiction.

'We felt we were battling against time with pretty limited resources trying to find out about crucial matters in his background that would turn events.

'It was stressful and I lay awake most nights thinking about this nightmare scenario and what more I could do legally to protect Simone.'

Mr Henry's team also discovered that the couple had signed over their NHS life insurance policies, worth around £60,000, to each other.

Unfortunately for Webster, a fire would prove to be the turning point for the detectives.

A childhood friend of Webster's, a fellow Scout, who had gone on to become a sergeant with Surrey Police, had written to Grampian Police in 2002 outlining his suspicion about the frequency of fires surrounding Webster. He was absolutely spot on.

Mr Henry said, 'We unearthed details of a small fire in a dustbin in 2003. Webster discovered the fire and he was regarded as a bit of a hero at the time for dealing with it. It was not a conclusive case but, based upon all the other fires, it was another one that Malcolm was there or thereabouts.'

That fire was at the Lorn & Islands District General Hospital, where Webster was working. He had blamed a patient for it, but a hospital consultant always doubted his account and spoke to police. Webster, police knew, had also started a fire at the home of a colleague in the west coast town, and had stolen a laptop from the hospital, although charges were later dropped.

Mr Henry said details of the fire were new information and just what they needed to allow them to issue Simone with an Osman letter.

Sometime after returning to Britain from New Zealand, Webster, a keen fisherman, had taken on the role of treasurer for the Oban and Lorn Angling Club. However, when he handed over the position to his successor Andy Macarthur, it was discovered that thousands of pounds were missing from the club's bank account.

'We were overdrawn by £70, but with membership fees there should have been around £4,500 in the bank,' Mr Macarthur said. 'Webster assured me he had paid numerous invoices on behalf of the club to the tune of about £6,000, but he hadn't. I and two other members reported it to the police, who wrote a letter to Webster.

'Sometime later I received a cheque for £6,000. He treated me like a fool. I believed there was always something about him.'

During his stay in the west coast town, he also claimed he had been a special forces major in the Saudi Arabian army, and he had a full desert uniform with major's insignia and a ballistic helmet, which he liked to show people. Police uncovered the uniform when executing a warrant to search his home after he was accused of stealing the money from the fishing club.

Mr Henry said, 'Webster was saying to various women that he had jobs in Saudi with the military. He hinted to people that he had some sort of involvement with the Special Forces there, like he was a medic for them. I think he just had to show them to people. It's quite safe to say that his claims to be involved with the military there were just part of the fantasy he was trying to establish. It was rubbish.'

Mr Henry added, 'He bought shirts from Bond Street, Harrods writing paper, all the best stuff from where gentlemen go – he had Savile Row suits.'

As well as the uniform, police found nine laptops, including the one stolen from the Lorn & Islands District General Hospital. A search of the computers uncovered emails which led police to another of Webster's women, American Brenda Grant, who went to Paris with him while he was pretending to have cancer treatment, of whom more later.

During the raid, officers also found an unlicensed shotgun, which Webster claimed was an antique. However, because of the raid, and Webster's expertise in explaining it away, Simone found herself a little hostile to the detectives, despite the wealth of evidence they were building against her husband-to-be. Even when they handed her the Osman letter, she couldn't connect the man she loved with the cold, manipulative stranger the police were warning her about.

Perhaps at this point, Felicity Drumm was the only person alive who could have sympathised or at least understood how she felt.

'I was in a state of total disbelief. I thought there must be some mistake because he was not married,' Simone recalled. 'It did not seem plausible in any shape or form that this could possibly relate to Malcolm. I had lots of questions but, legally, they couldn't answer them as it was an ongoing investigation.'

Simone was struggling to come to terms with the enormity

of her situation. After the confrontation with Webster, she even booked a room in a Dundee hotel for Webster.

The next day, against the advice of seasoned detectives sent to Oban to protect her, Simone and a friend met Webster in a supermarket car park in Dumbarton, Scotland.

Simone was horrified by the man who stood before her; he was not the man she knew. Or thought she knew. 'He was like a hunted man and very twitchy.'

She said her last goodbye to the killer in the garage forecourt. 'He said, "I love you." I filled up his car with diesel and gave him a hug. Somebody in a car behind tooted their horn for us to shift. I was angry as this was a major event in my life and I did not know if I would see him again.'

It seems incredible that she could feel like this, but she had given her heart to a man who she believed was about to die. It must have been a heart-rending decision to make in the first place. To then be told it was all a lie must have been almost too much to bear.

When Webster eventually admitted he had lied about the cancer, he did it over the phone.

'You could say that he was quite good at giving bad news over the phone,' Simone said. 'First, he phoned to tell me he had it, now he was phoning to tell me he didn't have it. The whole thing was just surreal and I did not know what to make of it. It is still hard to equate that with the person I knew. I don't for a second not believe it, having seen the change that came over him when I confronted him about his past, the substantial lies that I was told and the fact he could stick needles into himself to make me, and other people, believe a lie.

'But I don't hate him. There's no point in hating anybody because it's just wasted emotions.

'I think of him a bit like an alien species. I don't think he is wired up the same way as an average human being with the feelings and emotions we have.

'If you have not been involved with someone like him, then

it's hard to understand this. He was charming and that's what made him so plausible.'

Webster sent Simone a series of emails after his murderous scheme was interrupted by police.

In one, he wrote:

> I so wish that I hadn't lied to you about having leukaemia . . . and, of course, New Zealand, but I did. No plan, no game, just a crazy thing which I did which has resulted in the position we are in now.
>
> From my actions I have ruined what was in my heart the most perfect love.

So, even as Webster knew the noose was tightening, he was still taking the time to prepare a cover story, that of a philanderer rather than a murderer.

Simone later made a sinister and startling discovery. 'I found out, when I checked my life jacket, that my cylinder was punctured. The foil on my cylinder was punctured and I hadn't checked my life jacket since I'd sailed with him. Everybody else's life jackets were fine. So I have pretty much no doubt that the boat was the way it was gonna go. It sent a shiver up my spine.

'I am very fortunate. I had many, many guardian angels looking after me. One would never be enough for this guy.'

Exposed for the liar he was, aware he had lost Simone and unsure how much the police investigation had uncovered, Webster was weighing up his options.

He went to Aberdeen, visited Claire's grave, then bought a hosepipe and some Paracetamol to kill himself. However, according to his family, whom he called from a hotel to say goodbye, he could not end his own life.

His twin sister, Caroline Walters, drove to the hotel from her home in England to find him very much alive, and still telling lies about the money, Claire, Felicity and now Simone.

He also tried to have himself sectioned under the Mental Health Act after he walked into Aberdeen Royal Infirmary Accident and Emergency department in the early hours of 4 February 2008 and told staff he was considering killing himself. He also told a duty doctor that he had tried to take his own life with an overdose of insulin four days after Simone Banerjee confronted him over his lies. He was sent to mental health nurse Robert Mackie, and admitted he had bought Paracetamol to take his life but had backed out because it would be a 'prolonged and painful death'. The irony here is remarkable. Webster obviously felt he was an expert in administering painless deaths, but could not muster one for himself.

Detectives and a criminal profiler brought in to help the inquiry believed Webster is too arrogant to have gone through with it, although they felt that might change if he were ever imprisoned, where he was faced with no alternative.

Mr Mackie said, 'He said that the reason for the break-up was that he had an ex-wife and child in New Zealand whom he had not told Simone about, and that he had cancer when he did not. She had been very angry when she found out.'

Webster offered nothing by way of explanation for his actions, according to the nurse, who decided he was not genuinely suicidal and 'certainly not psychotic' but believed being admitted to hospital might help him escape his problems.

Knowing police were snapping at his heels, could Webster have been buying himself an alibi for any future court proceedings?

When he was refused admittance to the hospital, he drove to the south coast of England, stopping regularly to check for anyone following. They were, but he didn't see them.

Webster's brother Ian phoned Simone at 6.30 a.m. to tell her he had sent an email saying goodbye and that he was going to take his life.

Simone said, 'He said he had really enjoyed his time with

me, that he was sorry about the way things were at that point and that everything would come to me when he was gone. He also said he had loved me so much.'

A frantic Simone was unable to contact Webster as his phone was switched off. It wasn't until the next day that she heard he had been found alive in Cornwall.

Caroline and her husband had driven through the night to Bodmin in Cornwall after Webster. They found him sitting in his car in a car park. He had written the family goodbye notes. They managed to persuade him to return home with them. 'It was then that he said he didn't have leukaemia,' Caroline explained.

Naturally, she was utterly stunned when she discovered he had been lying all along, particularly as it was the very same cancer that had killed their mother. She said he had even visited their home wearing a hat. When he removed it he was bald, with shaved eyebrows. She said, 'I think Malcolm told me about his diagnosis just before my husband was diagnosed with multiple sclerosis. Malcolm telling me this was quite a shock.'

Webster maintained that he had lost his money in offshore investments and that he had been a fool, but not a killer. Simone and Felicity might beg to differ.

Now, as Webster hid in various addresses across the UK, his murderous spree was about to come to an end. Officers in Aberdeen, Oban, Glasgow and Auckland were joining forces to put an end to his criminal career.

Simone Banarjee had been lucky. She had Felicity Drumm to thank for it.

8

WEBSTER'S WOMEN

MALCOLM WEBSTER WAS NOT ALWAYS FAT, GREY AND bespectacled, and he didn't always waddle.

The image of him today is a world away from the one that the women in his life fell for. And there were plenty of them. So many, in fact, that a separate team had to be created within the Grampian Police inquiry just to collate them all and ensure they were all still alive and well.

Investigators had a whiteboard on one wall that read simply: 'Webster's Women'.

As detectives started to piece together the various lives of Malcolm Webster, they soon realised the monumental task that lay ahead. One of the most difficult aspects was sorting through the women, a job further complicated by the overlapping relationships. Police believe he seduced more than a dozen women after he murdered his wife and had up to three lovers on the go at any one time. As we know, he had at least three affairs while he was with Simone. It soon became clear to them that he had never been a one-woman man.

Quite how he managed to juggle all these relationships is anyone's guess, but it does show a highly organised, and manipulative, mind at work.

The women they knew about, who had come forward to

complain of foul play, and the ones they had warned about him were not so tricky. The problem lay with women nobody else knew about, the trysts. Every female Webster had been in contact with since his teenage years had to be traced and spoken to, in an effort to ensure that they were safe and that they did not have a complaint to make against him.

Imagine your entire sexual history laid bare on the cold walls of a room inside a police station. Everyone you ever slept with, lived with, worked with. In fact, every member of the opposite sex you ever had any contact with. That was the mammoth task officers were facing when they delved into Webster's past.

A profiler had labelled him a sociopath, and they had to do their utmost to ensure that they checked that these women were safe and well.

High-profile cases make headline news. From these cases, the best 'line' of that day's proceedings is broadcast into homes that evening and printed for the next day's readers. Behind these salacious titbits, there is the engine room of police work; that relentless drudgery of plodding on, checking off lists and putting everything in order, by the book.

When the groundwork is done, that's when you can see clearly what you have left to work with. Murder squad detectives can catch a killer red-handed standing over his victim and take a confession on the spot, but, if they don't take the necessary steps to prove the man they arrested is the man responsible, he will walk free. Whatever the failing in the inquiry, a defence lawyer will run through it faster than the officers can say Magna Carta.

The whiteboard entitled 'Webster's Women' may well have provided some light relief for the investigators during a long, drawn-out inquiry, but each and every female who was connected to Malcolm Webster in any way had to be found.

Webster had always been attractive to women. The photographs from both his weddings – to Claire and to Felicity – show a tall, slim, good-looking man, confidently looking into the lens. However, Webster had more than good looks – he was a charmer and, with his refined accent and good manners, he seemed the quintessential English gentleman, particularly to Claire, Felicity and Simone.

Simone, like Felicity, is a sensible, confident and successful woman from a happy, stable background, but, as she says, Webster 'is a very good actor and would give Colin Firth a run for his money. He was charming and that's what made him so plausible.'

A steady stream of women of a certain age had passed through Webster's life. Some of them would later count their blessings. They had all been duped, taken in, conned, but at least they were alive.

Detectives involved in the case were impressed by their bravery in stepping up to speak of their experiences. It could not have been easy. In some cases, they were admitting to trysts with him in the full knowledge that he was involved with someone else. Others did not know, and had been lied to like all the rest.

Webster rarely gave himself much time to get lonely. Within weeks of his young wife's tragic death, he had bought a yacht with the insurance money and invited mum-of-three Dorothy Allan, who worked with him, to spend the weekend with him.

Caroline McIntosh also enjoyed a trip on Webster's yacht, as well as an overnight hotel stay in Inverness and meals at the cottage he had shared with Claire.

Caroline, now 45, met Webster in August 1994 at Aberdeen Royal Infirmary where they both worked. She said 'weeks later' he invited her to his home for supper and she stayed overnight. However, Webster, who was also seeing another woman at the time, made sure that they never ventured into Aberdeen together and only Caroline's mother and brother-in-law knew about their relationship.

Their relationship ended when Webster left the UK to take up a job in Saudi Arabia just before Christmas 2004.

'He said he just wanted to get away before Christmas and New Year. After the year he had, he just wanted to get away,' Caroline said. 'It was a fairly casual relationship. We were going to see if we were going to have a proper relationship when he got back. I got the impression that he was coming back.'

Geraldine Oakley was another woman who had a brief relationship with Webster shortly after Claire's death. She would later tell the High Court at Webster's trial the incredible story of her short time with him.

She first met him in 1994, when she was in charge of computers at the hospital where routine samples of Claire's body were stored. Webster questioned her so intensively and persistently about whether there would be a second post mortem she almost alerted her superiors. Almost. Her boss, Dr James Grieve, was the scientist who would find the vital evidence that would prove Webster had murdered Claire.

When Webster told her he was leaving for Saudi, she raced to Dyce Airport in Aberdeen, hoping to say a final farewell. She never saw him there, or again.

Brenda Grant, now 49, of Kansas City, USA, had perhaps the longest association of all with Webster; they had an on-off relationship from 1995 to 2006, throughout Webster's marriage to Felicity and his engagement to Simone, although she knew nothing of either woman at the time.

Police traced Brenda after recovering the stolen laptops from Webster's home, and she believes she is lucky to be alive. She had no idea about Webster's sickening crimes but always thought he was 'too good to be true'.

When Webster was working in Saudi Arabia, he struck up a phone friendship with Brenda, an American colleague, although it wasn't until 1995, the year after Claire Morris's death, that they eventually met in person. They 'hit it off immediately, sparks flew'.

'If you see the pictures in the news now, you would wonder

how the heck he got all the women he did because he's not that attractive at this point,' Brenda said. 'In the early days when I first met him, he kind of looked like Sean Connery a little bit. He was a very romantic man, very charming, well travelled, humorous: a life-and-soul-of-the-party guy. He was a charmer.'

Despite their relationship coming to an end, they began sending each other emails in 2001.

Webster told her he was divorced and, in February 2006, the pair went on holiday to Paris, while Simone believed he was receiving cancer treatment. He also kept up the cancer charade with Brenda. 'Just before I met him in Paris he told me he had chronic lymphatic leukaemia. He said his spleen had been removed,' she said.

Ms Grant witnessed a heart-rending performance as Webster pretended to be terminally ill with leukaemia. During the trip they briefly rekindled their romance.

She said, 'I thought it might be the last time I would see him. When we met at the airport in Paris, he looked like someone who had been through chemo. One of the things that makes me angriest about the whole thing is that he played on people's emotions. I mean who in their right mind would pretend to have leukaemia?'

Brenda knew nothing of Simone Banarjee, back home in Oban, wondering how her man was coping with his chemotherapy treatment. 'He made me an unknowing participant in his deception. I had no idea he was involved with Simone. I distinctly remember a conversation in the hotel in Paris when he said he thought he was destined to be alone for the rest of his life.'

Brenda and Simone are now friends.

Brenda said, 'She's got the soul of an angel and it just pains me to think that I had an unknowing part of it, with the trip to Paris when she thought he was in London having treatment for his leukaemia.

'Obviously, I feel betrayed. When I look back I mainly have

fond memories and I hate to have them tarnished. At this point I have no idea what was true and what wasn't.

'I consider myself a fairly intelligent woman. Clearly, his performance was good enough or I wasn't paying enough attention to the signs.

'I nicknamed him "Mr OTT" as he was bigger than life and I always wondered if he was simply too good to be true. One of the reasons we parted when we did was because he was overwhelming; he was too much.

'I hope he gets what he deserves through the court system and that all the other women will move on as well.

'I feel lucky to be alive based on his previous history. I can remember travelling in Paris on back-roads with him in his vehicle which is what he appears to have used twice to do harm to other women in his life.

'So I feel pretty lucky to be here.'

Another former partner who has reason to feel lucky to be here is Christina Willis. Christina first met Webster in 2002 at the hospital in Oban where they both worked. He told her his first wife died in a car crash and that he had divorced his second wife because she had psychiatric problems.

Christina often had to loan him cash throughout their three-year relationship. She said he would often ask her to pay for things as it was 'the end of the month' for him. 'It wasn't unusual for him to suggest something that was going to involve expenditure, and then, when the time came, he didn't have the money.'

Despite sharing a home with him for much of their relationship, she never once saw a bank statement. Webster had them delivered to a post office box rather than their bungalow.

In fact, detectives and prosecutors would be left reeling at the level of deception employed by Webster. The PO boxes for bank and credit card statements, the constantly interplaying stories he had to remember depending on whom he was with that moment. They were impressed at the mental faculties, and disgusted by the clinical, cynical abuse of trust.

Christina and Webster had made out wills and power of attorney forms in each other's favour, but, perhaps sensing a more lucrative pay-off with Simone, Webster dumped Christina in 2005, claiming he had leukaemia.

She recalled, 'I was upset at the relationship coming to an end, but to be told that he had leukaemia was just awful news.'

He even asked her to lend him money shortly after he ended their relationship. 'He said he was having cash-flow problems. He had been telling me for some time that there were difficulties with payment from his employment.

'I was very, very worried about him being ill and I was concerned that these cash-flow problems were going to contribute to his ill health so I offered to lend him some money.'

As we have seen, Webster seemed to like taking his women to Claire's grave in Tarves. Webster had laid flowers at her grave with lover Catherine Brown, 45, and, as they stood there together, Catherine, perhaps expecting an emotional outpouring from Webster, was no doubt unnerved as he told her he had 'never had so much money' as he did following her death.

She told police, 'I remember him saying that after Claire died he had never had so much money, but he would always follow it up with something like, "But it will never bring her back", just to make it more palatable.'

Ms Brown, a nurse from Oban, Argyll, first met Webster in January 2005 when he was working as a moving and handling trainer at Lorn & Islands District General Hospital, although they did not become close until September that year, at the same time as he was grooming Simone. On 25 September, Webster, the consummate charmer, sent her an email that ended: 'Every time you see me you will see a man that loves you.'

She said that they were 'physically intimate' but their relationship was never sexual due to her Christian beliefs.

They stayed together at the Hilton Hotel in Ballater, Aberdeenshire, in December 2005 following the death of Webster's father, by which time he was involved in a relationship with Simone. He also took Catherine to his home, and also told her he had been diagnosed with advanced leukaemia.

Ann Hancock, another partner of Webster's, was also handed an Osman letter, warning her that her life was in danger, the same letter handed to Simone Banerjee. Detective Constable William Clarke travelled to Northampton Hospital three days before Christmas in 2008 to deliver the personal safety warning.

Ann, a physiotherapist who lives in Northampton, had jokingly nicknamed Webster Dr Death, unaware how close to the mark she had come. Ann gave him the moniker because he was studying for a degree in assisted death and euthanasia. During their investigation, cops found the official report into the activities of Dr Harold Shipman, who is believed to have killed over 200 patients in his care, on Webster's laptop. He claimed it was part of his studies for his degree.

Ann even joked about introducing him to her mum as 'Dr Death', but nobody was laughing when DC Clarke turned up at the hospital to hand over the warning letter.

DC Clarke said, 'Myself and my colleague attended at Miss Hancock's work. We didn't want to go to her home; we weren't sure if Mr Webster would be there. We took her into a room; there was no easy way to do this. We had to hand her the letter and let her read it.

'It was a couple of days before Christmas; you could just see her world falling apart in front of us. Initially, she didn't want to believe it. She took some time and had numerous questions, most of which we couldn't answer at the time.'

Ann met Webster in 2004 at a training course for manual handling advisers. She said he was a 'polite, charming and generous individual' and, several years later, following the end of her marriage, they began a relationship. They were in regular contact between October 2007 and early 2008, when he moved to Norwich.

She said they were preparing to buy a property together and she was shocked in December 2008 when police arrived at her work with a letter warning her about her partner. 'I didn't believe them. I just didn't believe it was true. I was stunned, I didn't believe the information they were saying or I was reading. It didn't match the person who I thought they were talking about.'

Ann received a card through the post within days of confronting Webster about the police warning.

> Whilst it might be and sound a strange thing to say I didn't mean to hurt you and I know that I did. I guess I just wanted to start a new life with you. I am so sorry to have hurt you. You won't have to hear from me again. I love you. I know that I have a strange way of showing that to you. Malcolm.

Webster had also brought up the subject of wills with Ann and advised her to have one written, although she said she had not taken him up on it. That may have been one of her wisest moves.

So how did Malcolm Webster manage to manipulate so many independent women and for so long? How did he convince so many women he loved them, that they were 'the one'?

Clearly, he had taken the time to develop his skillset in such a way that women were disarmed by him over a period of time. The warped genius of this is in its simplicity. Malcolm Webster knew women. He knew how to get inside their heads, and stay there, according to police and profilers. He knew what made them tick, how to press the right buttons to make them at ease in his company.

He had his plan, of course, but it was spread over such a vast period of time that each segment being slotted into place was almost imperceptible to the victims. He was a gentleman.

Surprisingly, most of the women in his life, those that were brought together in court to highlight his deceptions, had nothing bad to say about the time they spent with him.

While they spoke of having no knowledge of other women on the go when they were seeing him, none of the women in his life spoke of being spooked by him, or being shouted at by him, or assaulted by him.

Nobody said he was a violent lover, a selfish man, a philanderer. In fact, all of the women who spent time with Malcolm Webster had a good time.

How else was he able to meet women in London, in Paris, communicate by email with women in Saudi, the USA and England, all at the same time?

Some of them were in imminent danger all the time they were with him, but they only realised this when detectives arrived to tell them so. They were not so frightened of him, never unable to walk away.

In fact, in most cases, at first, they refused to believe what police were telling them. That's how good he was. Although perhaps he was being so good to them because he knew how bad he was going to be to them in the end.

The detectives who visited these women would regularly shake their heads in wonder as they made their way back to their vehicles. The reception they got ranged from incredulous laughter to quietly brooding resentment.

Women, some of whom were involved in the case, are still writing to Malcolm Webster to this day. He doesn't have their sympathy, as such, but they are looking for answers because in their own minds they simply cannot equate the man described to them by police with the man they loved.

They are seeking closure, but Webster, now stripped of all control, is trying to keep his last semblance of power, and is refusing to give it to them.

Webster loved money, and himself. But a scientist in the far north of Scotland was busy carrying out a series of experiments that could give his first wife Claire a voice, from beyond the grave.

9

THE SLIVER OF LIVER

DR JAMES GRIEVE WORKS WITH DEAD PEOPLE. HIS JOB, FOR the past 30 years, has been to make them talk. Some of them open up quickly to reveal their secrets, some take longer. Eventually, they all talk.

Getting Claire Morris to talk to him was one of the most difficult and ultimately rewarding chapters of his long and distinguished career.

Although humble, he is justifiably proud of what he achieved in the Webster investigation. Without his expertise, it would never have got off the ground and the Black Widower would still be free to lure his next victim, make his next killing, both financially and literally.

Dr Grieve's work on samples of tissue from the corpse of Claire Morris was hailed by detectives and prosecutors alike. As prosecuting QC Derek Ogg put it, 'Without him, we would have had nothing. Simple as that.'

By all means, call him a forensic pathologist, as he is one of the world's foremost experts in that field. Do not, however, make the mistake of calling him a detective. Crime scene investigators may solve crimes and confront the guilty on imported US TV shows, but the cold hard reality of Dr Grieve's work is that the body he is examining is someone's mother, father, brother, sister or child.

He is a scientist who is sometimes called to court to present his findings. Those findings are neutral, scientific, just how he likes them. They carry no assumption of guilt.

'I can only tell a court that a certain knife, with a certain serrated edge, was the knife that inflicted a deadly wound on a murder victim,' he explained. 'At no point do I ever say who was holding the knife. Not my job.'

Dr Grieve's evidence was absolutely crucial to the case but was delivered straight-down-the-middle, scientifically. As he says, he wasn't there to take sides.

However, he proved that Webster's first wife Claire had drugs in her system on the night she died. How he proved it, 13 years after the event, is the stuff of a Discovery Channel documentary. It is an extraordinary story of science and scientists pushing the boundaries of their chosen spheres. For Dr Grieve, it was simply the end process after a request from Grampian Police to 'see what I could do'.

For the relatives of Claire Morris, for Felicity, Simone and all the others, it was the one piece of evidence that would ensure their nightmare was over.

Grieve is a remarkably likeable fellow who has plied his trade over decades and thousands of corpses. In his world, he is surrounded by death, the tissues of the dead, stacked high all around him. He explains death. He has the gait of a scientist too, slightly stooped from too much time at a microscope, and with the bushy greying eyebrows that belie the sharpness of his mind.

Whether he accepts it or not, his evidence in the Malcolm Webster case was one of the critical cornerstones of the police case. He may well play down his role to that of scientist, as he should, but without him the case would have been lost.

Dr Grieve's no-nonsense science proved malice aforethought on the part of Malcolm Webster.

As the head of forensic pathology at Aberdeen University, he has watched his department grow over the decades in keeping with the growth spurts in his chosen field.

A reserved man, he keeps his own counsel and still feels slightly uneasy that the evidence he gave had been reported so widely as the smoking gun in the Webster probe.

In fact, he even admits to being slightly annoyed that so much weight was placed on his evidence by the press reporting, and abhors the phrase 'sliver of liver', as it came to be known in the tabloids.

However, it was a tiny sliver of Claire Morris's liver, held in storage since 1994, first under a glass plate then in a block of wax, that helped him succeed. That tiniest part of a loved one, a sample stored as part of a routine storage process conducted after all fatal road accidents in this country, when tiny segments from all the main organs are harvested and stored.

'This whole "sliver of liver" was reported almost too heavily, and I wasn't too keen to speak to the press about the matter at the time,' Dr Grieve admitted. 'The liver analysis was not the central part of the case at all. The case was all about very thorough investigation and all the superb evidence that was gathered by a huge team of detectives. It was truly massive, on an epic scale.

'I'll be truthful about this; one of the things that worries me about all of this is how people perceive forensics because of what they've watched on TV. The truth is that forensic pathology is not the most important part of any case in terms of prosecution.

'We are meticulous in our examinations and we can sometimes come away with certain insights but we are not the people who say the accused was the person wielding the weapon, as it were.

'The analysis of the liver came in the early days of the investigation when there was clearly quite substantial suspicion over what had actually happened to Claire Morris. The problem was to justify opening an investigation that would be unique in Scottish legal history.

'It would also be a police investigation that would be hugely expensive for Grampian Police and they had to have justification for proceeding. They asked us if there was anything we could do, that was back in 2007.

'All we had were these little pieces of material, samples, from Claire's body, so we attempted what had not been attempted before. We did it on spec and came up with a result, a 92 per cent chance that there was Temazepam in Claire's liver.'

His reasoning is purely scientific. He was only 92.4 per cent sure. A prosecutor will take that return every time. A scientist should never, and, typically, he added, 'As a scientist, you immediately realise that leaves an 8 per cent chance that there was not.

'When we reported those findings to the police, they told us that was enough for them to have a very close look at what they were now very suspicious of. Much was made of the liver sample in court as it attracted the interest of the press and the people prosecuting, but we could never replicate that result, and we tried.

'We had to create a whole new process which had never been done anywhere in the world before, and it only worked once.

'There were so many variables, from the solubility of Temazepam to the washing of the samples, which you need to do to get a histological section that can be studied.

'All I can say is we got it but it was very disappointing that we could not replicate it. Temazepam dissolves readily in chloroform, which was used to "fix" the samples.

'But solicitors do not care about the science, do they? They got the one 92 per cent result and said, "Thanks very much."

'I should say I'm in no way anxious about that result; it was a proper and correct outcome and everything was conducted properly, but as a scientist I wanted to repeat it but couldn't. We didn't have enough by way of samples.'

A measure of the respect shown by Dr Grieve to his trade is

his reluctance to jump to conclusions, or indeed to take any credit. 'The case actually hung on all the other evidence, which was very strong,' he insisted.

'In my opinion the liver test is unimportant except that it allowed Grampian Police to press ahead with an investigation that proved very fruitful. I have no problem with the result. It's really more about how Webster managed to get away with it for so long.'

The skillset required to achieve that 92 per cent is what Dr Grieve does not dwell upon. He is a confident man, confident enough not to have to blow his own trumpet, yet his work over the decades, and on the Webster case, has earned him a deserved reputation as one of the world's leading specialists in his field.

His involvement in the Webster case, however, was almost too close for comfort.

He added, 'I have knowledge of other people that Webster duped, including one woman who worked for me within the biochemistry department.

'Webster befriended her just after he murdered Claire. The woman, a computer manager, was at one time very close to the door of my office fully intending to knock on my door and tell me she had concerns about him. As it turned out, she took cold feet, as it were, and walked away from my office door. She was that close to dropping him in it, way back then, in 1994.'

The woman in question was Geraldine Oakley, who had a brief affair with Webster in the months following his first wife's death and slept with him on the first anniversary. But Webster may have targeted her for his own ends.

Geraldine, of Cruden Bay, Aberdeenshire, became Webster's lover months after Claire's death and, as the relationship developed, she began to suspect he had killed her. She has always lived with the regret of not knocking on the door of her then boss, Dr Grieve, and sharing her concerns with him.

Geraldine, now 50, said she began to suspect Webster because of his interest in whether a second autopsy was going to be carried out on Claire.

As Dr Grieve explained, she was outside her boss's door on at least three occasions, so concerned was she about the questions Webster was asking her, such as where Claire's tissue samples were stored.

Dr Grieve added, 'She was working around the samples taken from Claire's body at the time, and had access to these. Had she knocked on my door back in 1994 and voiced her concerns, I would still have had Claire's bloods and could have run a full drug screening.

'That would have revealed Temazepam and the game would have been up for Malcolm Webster. At that time, we only screened for alcohol, although it was just a few years later that drugs screening was introduced in all fatal road traffic accidents.

'In 1994, the illicit-drugs scene was not nearly as developed as it is now. We have had 45 illicit drugs deaths to date this year [as of August 2011]; in 1994, at the time of Claire's death, we had nothing like that. A lot of what we do as pathologists is intelligence driven so at that time we would not be routinely screening for drugs.

'In 1994, it would have been an alcohol screen alone. Had Claire died two or three years later, there would have been a routine drugs test on samples and he would have been discovered.

'It's incredible how lucky he was when you consider those two things alone, either that or he was able to manipulate those around him so well. He was very lucky he was not caught back then. This relationship he began with Geraldine happened quickly after Claire's death. Did he want someone on the inside, as it were, to tell him about tests being done on Claire's samples? Who knows? That's exactly what worries me. He's a highly intelligent criminal, and Geraldine, at that time, had to do with computers on which that very material from Claire was recorded.

'In 1994, it was very early in terms of computing records so I don't think much of it would have been on computer then, as I was always very wary of tissue samples and how secure they were.

'Ill fortune, like the rain, falls on the good and bad alike and, in a hospital with 5,000 staff, there's every chance we hold samples of relatives of staff who work here.

'That's why I always took the view to keep them as secure as possible.'

Detectives were aware of this relationship. It chilled everyone on the investigating team and hardened their resolve. A man prepared to go to such lengths would do anything to evade capture.

Dr Grieve added, 'Did he strike up this friendship as he believed the data related to Claire would be on computer? In the full knowledge that he had drugged Claire, perhaps he wanted to know if such an analysis had been done and what the results were?

'And who better to engage than the woman in charge of the computers within pathology? Maybe he was just attracted to her. It will forever be an interesting and worrying case for me because of that aspect alone. Quite chilling.'

Dr Grieve embarked on one of the most interesting chapters of his fascinating career with a simple question to expert colleagues at the American Academy of Forensic Sciences, where he was visiting to give a series of lectures. He outlined the details of the case, told them what the police had asked him to achieve, and asked them, 'Am I being stupid?'

He added, 'In our reports put before the court at the Webster case, it is quite clear what we did, how we did it and what the outcomes were. In my career, I have been totally truthful, very careful and completely unbiased, but it was a gargantuan effort on the part of toxicology to achieve what we did with Claire's tissue samples.

'First of all, we had to get rid of all the wax that holds the tissue samples so that the sample can go through the machines we use. I happened to be visiting the American Academy of Forensic Sciences at the time and asked colleagues for their views. I actually asked if what I was planning to do was stupid. Their reaction was typical: "It's never been done before so you might as well have a go."

'An old professor of pathology once told me, "Nothing's too stupid to try." So I tried. And it worked.

'But, given we had very little material to work with, we weren't about to waste it without knowing what we were looking for.

'It is a normal part of any post mortem that some tissue samples are retained. We usually take postage stamp-size pieces of every major organ. Indeed, that was what we had in terms of Claire Morris's material.

'Prior to 2000, this was done routinely without any relatives knowing about it, given the obvious sensitivities of the subject. The Scottish law on tissue retention is wiser than English law. The Scottish Parliament, after much consultation, recognised these samples – some of which here at Aberdeen date back as far as the 1930s – are a vital resource both now and in the future.

'We have already been working with geneticists and examining cases where we can tell youngsters if they have the same DNA fault as their grandparent who died of a heart attack at 33. That's because we have samples of their grandparent and can go check the DNA for the abnormality present in Granddad to see if it is present in the related youngster. Thirty-five years ago, nobody realised there was even a familial link. That, in essence, is why retaining samples is so vital.

'You take a little piece of tissue, one centimetre by one

centimetre and four or five millimetres thick. That material is placed into a formaldehyde solution called "fixing". Without doing this, it would putrefy and degenerate.

'From that, you have to be able to cut a very fine piece of tissue, five microns, or 5000th of a millimetre, which you stain with a variety of stains. This process is simply essential in the diagnosis of most diseases.

'In order to be able to cut such a fine slice, you need to have something relatively solid. For the past 150 years, the best way to do that was to put the sample into a block of paraffin wax. That takes the water and the fats out of the cells and replaces it with wax. You now have a little block which is roughly two centimetres by one-and-a-half centimetres and about seven millimetres in depth.

'When we want to use it, we wash it and cut off our section for analysis. The glass slides we place them under are stored in drawers. Glass is heavy and deteriorates when exposed to light so we can't keep them forever. In a year we'll deal with 40,000 cases and when you take 10 samples from each person that means 400,000 pieces of glass. It's a huge amount of space and a heavy weight. These are the things nobody really wants to think about, but there are practicalities at play in our field.

'At one hospital, the entire storage area had to be relocated from a room above a cellar as the collective weight of these tiny glass slides was making the floor sag. We had to get rid of them after 10 or at most 20 years because of the degradation. The new little wax block, although bigger, is much lighter and we can keep these securely.

'Our store goes back to the 1930s, we don't like getting rid of things. Every block has a patient number which is impregnated into it. They are then stored in boxes of 100 at a time. We have a vast cellar storage area that contains 10 to 15 years' worth of samples and another off-site secure storage area that has the rest.

'At the Royal Infirmary here, we lost some blocks because of a heat problem from a fire. We lost a couple of years' worth of records as the wax melted.

'That made me think about Webster and his penchant for fire. I have no doubt that, had he known it would be a problem for him and had he known the location of Claire's samples, he would not have hesitated to act. It would not have survived. He would have burned the storage facility down.

'In fact, when the investigation restarted, the blocks containing the samples from the Claire Morris case were kept in my safe in the office, which is fireproof. I took the decision to do that, given the suspicions at the time. It was most definitely the right thing to do.

'We worked on these tiny samples without knowing if there would still be trace elements of anything found within them. It had been so long, and the process of getting them ready for analysis was intrusive to the sample and could potentially wipe anything in there before we could even examine it.

'But, somehow, we managed to get to the result we did. We were elated at that.'

Dr Grieve explained that he and toxicologist colleague Dr Duncan Stephen used part of Claire's liver tissue because the liver is considered a primary site of drug metabolism in the body.

In court, Dr Stephen explained that he normally worked with 1 gram of liver, but in this case was using one-thousandth of that. That gives some indication of the parameters within which the two men were working.

Dr Stephen said that one of the problems he faced was that chloroform was used in 1994 to wash the liver. He revealed a significant amount of Temazepam would have been dissolved in the process of washing the liver sample.

The work carried out by Dr Grieve and others within the department was so groundbreaking that papers are being prepared to put before the wider forensic toxicology community.

He added, 'We managed to prove that Claire Webster had drugs in her liver at the time of her death. But we didn't prove it absolutely. And no scientist likes that.'

The Webster case has been the most interesting in a long and varied career for Dr Grieve. But it is, for him, just another case.

For the victims, he is a scientific hero. Without him there could not have been a reopening of the inquiry into Claire's death. The procurator fiscal at Aberdeen would not have allowed it.

Only by showing that drugs were in samples of her liver was permission granted to spend the millions of pounds required to bring the Black Widower to justice.

For Dr Grieve, life goes on, this life of dealing with death in all its varied guises. 'I'm not the usual issue of forensic pathologist and I would like to retire when I'm 60, in a couple of years' time. I can say that it's been a very pleasing and interesting paper round, but I wouldn't say it was anything other than hard. In over 20 years here, I've never used up my annual holiday entitlement!

'Webster does fascinate me though. I remember there was much made of Malcolm Webster's blood pressure being normal and his pulse low immediately after the accident which killed Claire. If you had just been in an accident and your own dear wife had died, you would be in a state of considerable anxiety. In fact, you would probably never get behind the wheel of a car again. I know I wouldn't.

'It beggars belief that he could walk away from a scene of horror like that and go on, days later, to buy himself a new 4X4.

'Yes, I can safely say Webster has been the single most interesting case. The challenges involved, the man himself, the story of his crimes, and the fact that we were able to help, gives me no small sense of satisfaction at a job well done. He tried to manipulate people around him for his own gain, and he should pay the price for that.

'My part in his downfall, as it were, is a relatively small one, but I am glad we were able to provide the means to go after him.

'And I'm very glad, having heard all the evidence about the fire-raising all over the world, that I locked those little pieces of Claire Morris in the office safe.'

10

'DID HE DO IT?'

THE HAIRS ON THE BACK OF MY NECK STOOD TO ATTENTION as I pressed the mobile phone more firmly to my ear in an effort to block out the city noise around me.

The call had rooted me to the spot on a bustling pavement in the heart of Glasgow's west end.

People were spilling out of the nearby tube station and into Ashton Lane for Friday-night drinks. Glasgow was alive. It was March 2008, and it was the first time I had ever heard the name Malcolm Webster.

'Can you say that again?'

My source on the other end of the phone was a senior police officer. Very senior. He didn't call often but when he did it invariably led to an exclusive story.

What I thought I'd heard him say had stopped me in my tracks, en route to join the Friday-night masses for a few beers. And when the hairs on the back of my neck bristled like that it was always time to listen carefully. That didn't happen too often either. After almost two decades of unearthing hard news and investigating criminals for Scotland's biggest-selling Sunday newspaper, not a lot stopped me dead in the street.

The source, who must remain anonymous for obvious reasons, raised his voice over the crackling line. 'We have a man called Malcolm Webster; we think he poisoned and murdered his first wife in Aberdeen, then tried the same thing with his second wife in New Zealand, and we have had to warn another woman in Oban that we believe her life may be in danger. He's been out there doing this, along with a series of fires we can link to him, for over ten years. And we can't find him.'

For the first time in my career, I was stunned into silence.

My source went on to say that the murder of Webster's first wife had taken place in 1994, some 14 years previously, and that new forensic science techniques had been invented to find traces of a drug in liver samples kept since her death. They had just received the results. Claire Webster had been sedated prior to the crash being staged and her husband had apparently got away with murder. Until now.

He told me they were dealing with a man who killed for money.

Chillingly, he added, 'We need to find this guy, but more importantly we need to get the message out there about him. He was recently living in Oban with a woman, and we had to go and tell her she was in danger. He was engaged to be married to her. She had signed everything over to him and he was planning to take her out. It was exactly the same MO as the first two women.

'The decision to warn her was made at the highest level and is a first in my career as a police officer. That's how serious we are about him.'

Malcolm Webster, an ordinary, nondescript name that appeared to fit the seemingly nondescript man who answered to it. It was a stunning telephone call.

I returned to the office, found some records of his living in Aberdeen and lots of local newspaper cuttings about the accident which claimed the life of his first wife Claire. There was also a smaller news story about a fire at their home, which I shuffled to the back of the pile at that time. In the fullness of time, that little fire would come to be as important to police investigators as the murders themselves in establishing a pattern of behaviour at Webster's trial.

Digging through the online cuttings system, I discovered a small story from earlier that week, in a local paper in Aberdeen, in which Grampian Police had issued an appeal for information about a car crash linked to the one I was now investigating as a potential murder dressed to look like an accident.

Grampian Police had sent letters to locals in the area appealing for information about a crash which happened just weeks before the fatal collision – the 'dry run' ahead of the fatal accident staged by Webster. They also asked to speak to anyone who might have spotted Webster in the area in the weeks leading up to the crash.

A Grampian Police spokesman said at the time, 'We can confirm we are reviewing the circumstances surrounding a road traffic collision on 28 May 1994, where a woman tragically died.

'This review is at a very early stage and, as is usual in such circumstances, the Crown Office and Procurator Fiscal Service is fully aware of the matter.'

The police had been scant with details, and the story had sunk without trace.

Now we were about to print the story that cold-case cops on two continents were linking up to prove that Webster had drugged and murdered his first wife, tried to do the same to his second bride and that a third woman had been warned about him by worried detectives.

On the surface, Malcolm Webster was an upstanding member of society. A softly spoken middle-class man making his way in life with a tragic tale to tell of his first wife's death. He was a male nurse, a carer, the kind of man who gives newspaper lawyers sleepless nights, and we had to be right in what we were about to say about him.

The fact that Grampian Police had shown their hand to

some extent with the appeal for witnesses to the accident gave me some comfort, but a call to the press office soon changed that. My questions were met with a stern 'no comment'. Not even an off-the-record briefing or steer to tell me I was on the right track.

Strathclyde Police denied all knowledge and directed my enquiries to Grampian, thereby closing the loop, with me on the outside of it.

By this time, photographers were in place at homes across the UK and we were taking steps to trace his second wife, Felicity Drumm, in a place called Takapuna in New Zealand. I needed someone to speak, on the record, or there would be no story.

I had also managed to find a couple of email addresses and a mobile-phone number for Webster and was routinely calling this and emailing him for comment.

I found the number for Takapuna Police in Auckland, New Zealand, on the web and decided to place a call. It was 9 a.m. in Scotland, 8 p.m. there. The press office was closed, according to the message, and I waited for a duty officer to pick up the telephone, which had looped through to the station's control room.

When the bored cop on the late shift 12,000 miles away finally answered, and I told him why I was calling, his response lifted me out of my chair and brought a huge smile to my face. 'Yeah, I remember old Malcolm, I worked on that case.'

No matter how strong your facts are, there are times when you still need that little bit of luck, and here he was, an officer of the New Zealand Police Force, confirming one of the most remarkable stories I had ever heard, from all that way away, in a little police station in Takapuna, Auckland, population less than 3,000.

He confirmed, after tapping some keys, that Malcolm Webster was a wanted man: for setting a series of fires at the home of his second wife's parents, and at a home they were in

116

the process of buying. 'There is also an international arrest warrant in place for stupefying his wife Felicity Drumm and for the subsequent car crash, as well as for the fires here.'

As I took a shorthand note of the official statement from him, I noticed the office had gone strangely quiet.

When I replaced the receiver, the news editor was immediately by my side. 'Get ready to be happy,' I told him.

We had enough to run a story. The picture desk had managed to find a photograph of Webster and first wife Claire, taken on their wedding day. Just a matter of months after they posed for that happy portrait, she was dead, drugged and murdered by the man standing next to her in his smart Highland dress jacket.

The black and white image showed a happy and proud young woman smiling out to the world, standing beside a much taller new hubby. He looked superior in the image, happy too, but with a certain smugness. It was the first time I had laid eyes on Malcolm Webster. He looked ordinary. Like you or me.

We approached Simone Banarjee in Oban, and she told us she did not want to comment and to contact the police who were dealing with it. Again, it was another confirmation of police involvement. From the information I had been given, we also knew that tests had been carried out on the liver samples retained ever since the first post mortem on his first wife Claire, after the 1994 crash, and that these, together with the copycat accident in New Zealand, were helping police build a prosecution case against this homicidal husband.

Grampian Police eventually released a statement and confirmed that their forensic experts had found traces of a sedative drug in Claire's liver. That gave my editor the confidence to run the story. The next day, splashed across the front page of the biggest-selling Sunday newspaper in the country, ran the questioning headline: 'Did He Do It?'

'Two wives poisoned, one murdered?'

Webster maintained his silence, despite concerted efforts to get a statement from him. We didn't at that time know his whereabouts but he responded to email requests with one-line 'no comment' replies.

Within minutes of our first edition hitting the streets, the Internet came alive with it. The BBC immediately ran it across their news sites and the story pinged all around the globe within hours.

The New Zealand media dispatched news crews to Scotland and rang up for interviews. It went global very quickly.

But I knew there was more. I felt Webster was a man worth pursuing. He was to become the most interesting criminal I have ever investigated and worthy of the particular interest paid to him by hundreds of police officers spread across the globe.

My original source had told me something in that first call that meant I had to keep digging. He had been labelled a sociopath by a criminal profiler allowed access to the files in the earliest days of the investigation. So what else was he responsible for? How many more victims were there? Where had he been in the intervening years?

At the beginning of the inquiry, Grampian Police failed to join the dots in the Webster case, despite being repeatedly asked to do so by their colleagues in New Zealand.

Senior officers in Auckland knew about the crash that killed his first wife and were hunting for Webster in connection with a copycat second crash. Grampian detectives were slow to respond, slow to reopen the case and, according to Auckland cops, seemingly didn't want to know.

It was almost seven years after the New Zealanders issued the international arrest warrants that Grampian finally woke up to the case and began a cold-case review. The task ahead of them was monumental and was second in scale only to the infamous Lockerbie inquiry, when terrorists bombed Pan Am 103 out of the sky over the Scottish border town in December

1988, killing 270 people. Eleven of those were Scottish residents of the border town who were killed by falling plane debris.

Reopening Webster's case would mean locating and re-interviewing witnesses years after the event. The original witness statements had been lost, and officers who attended at the time were retired or had moved to pastures new.

The most difficult aspect for Grampian was that this case was always going to be about circumstantial evidence. There was no smoking gun, no DNA at the scene, and no murder weapon. The victim was dead, her relatives knew little that could help in the case and they only had the tiniest samples of Claire's remains kept since the original post mortem into her death.

They had to try to establish if she had been sedated prior to being placed in the car driven into a verge by Webster. That had never been done before. Forensic colleagues would have to invent new techniques to achieve this and it took over two years to accomplish.

Webster, meanwhile, had walked into a police station in England after the story appeared and politely enquired if the police were looking for him.

He was interviewed, before being released without charge. As detectives got their first look at their prime suspect, he repeatedly answered 'no comment' to their questions.

He was ordered to report to his local police station every day while their enquiries continued. They didn't want to lose him again, not when the stakes were so high.

He never missed an appointment at the local police office, and lived with family, as detectives attempted to piece together the jigsaw of his crimes in a way that a jury could understand.

Cops in New Zealand flew to Scotland to help and the case was the first of its kind in Scots law where a crime committed in the southern hemisphere could be tried in a Scots court.

The reason was simple. The money Webster stole from

second wife Felicity Drumm in Auckland, almost £200,000, was sent to Webster's Scottish bank account. That gave them jurisdiction.

Webster complained to the Press Complaints Commission and to the chief constable of Grampian Police over my story. In his letter to the press watchdog, he claimed the story was a 'pack of lies' and that he would take further action if no apology was forthcoming.

He also complained to Grampian's chief constable that someone within his force had leaked information on the case to me and to New Zealand detectives.

One year later, I was voted Reporter of the Year at the Scottish Press Awards and the revelations about Malcolm Webster were highlighted by judges as the best story of the year. As I was being patted on the back by colleagues, detectives were finally putting the finishing touches to a court case that would shock Scotland and beyond and make legal history as the longest prosecution of its kind in the country.

The length of time that passed between the original telephone call from my source and the story appearing was less than 24 hours. I realised immediately that it was just one of many days, weeks and months I would spend tracking and writing about Malcolm Webster.

Despite batting my enquiries away with one- and two-line emails, Webster was far more talkative to New Zealand press when the story first broke.

In a series of astonishing emails to newspapers there, he protested his innocence, but added that he didn't care if nobody believed him.

It's possible he had an eye on what his son would read or be told about him in the coming weeks, months and years, and had attempted to get his own twisted version of events 'out there'.

At the time of emailing news groups down under, the

worldwide probe into his murderous affairs was well under way, but not complete. The arrogance behind the words employed in his emails is incredible, knowing what we now know about him.

He denied trying to kill Felicity in the Auckland car crash and accused her and her parents of trying to turn his young son against him.

> My first wife's death was a tragic event and there is not a single day that I don't think of her. She was the most perfect person I have ever met, I really don't care if people believe that or not.
>
> I will be more than happy if the police wish to speak to me but I am not suspected of killing anyone.

He described his relationship with Felicity as 'different' in a cold-hearted dig at her.

> I know that we both had issues that we brought into the relationship, and I am sure that we both learned things about each other that we didn't know when we lived in the Middle East.
>
> However . . . there was no crash whatsoever. We came off the main highway in the middle of the day and pulled up on the grass verge as there was a vibration with the car. There was no injury whatsoever to Felicity.
>
> A simple check will confirm this and there was no damage to the car.

He also complained that he had tried to come back to the country to fight for custody of his son but his entry had been blocked.

> I spoke to my lawyer on the phone at the airport and even suggested that the police come and interview me; however,

they didn't bother and I had to return to the UK. There seems little point in putting charges to the court if you are not allowing the person to enter the country.

Since then I have not been allowed a visa, lost a judicial review, but far worse than that is not being able to see my son.

I am sure that Felicity and her father have explained to my son that his father is a terrible person. If I had been guilty of any of the allegations that Felicity and her father had made, I would have had no interest in trying to return to New Zealand.

I returned because I knew then, and still do, that the allegations were not true. I am not asking you to believe me, I have nothing to hide. I am still waiting to see if the police wish to speak to me.

I hope that Felicity is happy and I wish her well, but I believe that there have been some very strange practices undertaken with regards to the allegations made against me. Despite suggestions, I am not and have never been 'in hiding' from either the British or New Zealand Police.

In fact, I was fully aware that Grampian Police were undertaking a review into the tragic death of my wife Claire. They are fully aware of where I am staying, and have my mobile number.

For the record, I attended my local police station, I explained who I was and on checking their records they showed no interest whatsoever in me. I do not have a criminal record.

This has been a difficult time. I remember vividly the events of that terrible evening of May 27, 1994.

However, there has been a lot of 'misinformation' made by other parties and this has resulted in some quite outrageous statements.

Webster went on to insist that he had arranged to return to New Zealand in 2000:

> with the full knowledge of all those concerned, and despite suggestions from my wife's family that I would be arrested on my return.
>
> I was detained at Auckland airport and was then refused entry, following a statement by New Zealand Police, and I therefore returned to the UK.
>
> I then applied for a visa from New Zealand High Commission in London and this was refused, for reasons unknown.

At the time Webster's heartless email was printed, Felicity's mum Margaret said, 'We can't take any more shocks. He is an accomplished liar.'

After all the outrages committed by Webster upon them, they had to put up with his attempts to smear Felicity through the press, labelling their relationship as simply 'different'.

As Webster was making his claims, the team of detectives from Grampian Police were quietly going about their business. Witnesses were traced all over the world, in some cases with the help of the FBI and Interpol, and statements taken. Perhaps Malcolm Webster felt it was a case that could never be taken to court, given the vastly different jurisdictions; perhaps that's what gave him the confidence to speak out in print. Either way, his own remarks about the crashes would come back to haunt him in a Scottish courtroom as he faced a jury of his peers.

11

A CASE TO ANSWER

IT BEGAN IN THE SNOWBOUND DEPTHS OF THE WORST
winter on record and ended on a bright summer's day. It was a
murder, fraud and arson trial rolled into one, with no DNA
evidence or smoking gun to rely upon. There wasn't even a
body to speak of.

The trial of Malcolm John Webster began on 1 February
2011 and lasted three months and 18 days, the longest trial of
a single accused person in Scottish legal history. Evidence was
led of crimes committed on the other side of the world, in a
small satellite of Auckland called Takapuna, New Zealand,
population under 3,000.

It had taken years to get here and involved co-operation and
information-gathering from police forces across the globe.

When prosecutor Derek Ogg QC accepted the case, he knew
there were challenges ahead, not least of which was the scarcity
of hard evidence. After walking into the files room, he was, for
a moment, unsure of where to even start. And Ogg has a
photographic memory. There was an Everest of evidence. Now
all he had to do was lead the jury through it.

This was a case, Ogg believed, where he had to prove that
nobody on earth could be as unlucky as Malcolm Webster.
That, coupled with some ground-breaking investigative

techniques and reconstructions, together with a money trail that implied guilt and malice aforethought, would, he believed, be enough to secure conviction.

When you included the evidence of the fires that followed Webster all over the globe, the case was compelling.

However, as the esteemed QC knew only too well, there is no such thing as a certainty in court.

He had a black widower in his sights, a man who killed for money. The charge sheet ran to 11 pages. His second victim, Felicity Drumm, had signed a witness statement that was 150 pages long. However, the man in the dock had steadfastly maintained his silence throughout interviews.

Murder, attempted murder, lies and bigamy. There was a series of fire-raisings and attempted fire-raisings, the drugging of victims, as well as the theft of vast sums of money in ongoing complicated frauds.

All of this dated back to at least 1993. In February 2011, could the Crown pull it all together into a cohesive narrative? Could it be told in a way that the jury could follow? A way that would ensure guilty verdicts?

It was alleged that Webster's campaign of terror for financial gain began with the drugging of first wife Claire. He gave her Temazepam soon after their wedding in September 1993 at Aberdeen's King's College Chapel. Prosecutors believe he could have started drugging her on their honeymoon night. He allegedly gave her the drug, causing her to lose consciousness, on 27 May 1994.

The Crown claimed he then carried her to their 4X4 Daihatsu jeep, and drove it down an embankment near Kingoodie, Aberdeenshire, before setting it alight, knowing Claire was inside.

He was also charged with pretending to four people that he was alone in the car when it crashed, and therefore charged with preventing Claire from being rescued.

The indictment also claimed Webster persuaded Claire to

take out 11 insurance policies before he killed her. He was also alleged to have fraudulently cashed in a series of insurance policies, amounting to £208,815, as well as receiving widower's pension payments of £10,439 when he was not eligible for them.

Webster married Felicity Drumm in Auckland, New Zealand in April 1997. He was accused of attempting to murder Felicity by giving her the drug Clonazepam over a 30-month period at locations in Aberdeenshire, Saudi Arabia, the United Arab Emirates and New Zealand.

It was also alleged that Webster tried to kill Felicity in a car crash in February 1999 in Auckland, New Zealand. The indictment alleged he put petrol, newspapers and a lighter in the car before driving it at high speed on an Auckland road, careering down an embankment and hitting a tree. He was charged with forging Felicity's signature on insurance policies before the alleged murder bid in an attempt to fraudulently obtain £514,026 and £242,000 in separate insurance payouts.

It was further alleged that he persuaded Felicity to leave him everything in her will. He was also accused of asking Felicity to open two joint bank accounts with him and fraudulently taking more than £35,000 from her.

Webster was said to have set fire to paperwork and an armchair at a property in Auckland – the home of Felicity's parents – in a bid to cover his tracks.

It was also alleged that, in 2004, Webster met a third woman, Simone Banarjee, at a hospital in Oban, Argyll, and falsely told her he was free to marry.

He also told her he had terminal leukaemia, it was claimed on the indictment. It was also alleged he asked Simone to pay for their wedding and induced her to make a will leaving him her entire estate.

Even before it got off the ground, there were serious questions regarding jurisdiction to be addressed. How could Webster, they asked, be tried in Scotland for crimes he had committed in New Zealand?

Ogg produced a masterstroke here. Even Webster's own solicitor John McLeod acknowledged as much. 'They were very clever in this regard as they ran the case as an ongoing fraud. Because Webster had moved the stolen money from Felicity's account in New Zealand to his own Clydesdale Bank account in Aberdeen, that gave them jurisdiction. Had he not moved the money to Scotland, he would probably never have been tried here. Without the New Zealand evidence, it would have been a much more difficult case to prosecute. So yes, a masterstroke is not an exaggeration for what happened there.'

Ogg and his team had to wade through information gleaned in an inquiry that had lasted over five years and saw officers from Grampian Police travel the globe to obtain witness statements, thousands of them. Some of them would come to be vital, some not so much. But everything had to be read.

Officers from New Zealand had travelled to the UK to assist with the inquiry and some would be required to give evidence. Even keeping the witness list at a manageable level was proving to be a gargantuan task. Defence solicitor John McLeod had to fly to New Zealand and interview no fewer than 60 witnesses ahead of the trial.

There was enough to convict, and Ogg was in no doubt over Webster's guilt. However, as he sat trying to piece together the biggest jigsaw he had ever taken on, he knew one wrong move would spell disaster for an inquiry that had cost a sizeable chunk of Grampian Police's annual budget over the previous years.

The trial gripped the public imagination and was beamed nightly into homes in Scotland, New Zealand and Australia via live newscasts from outside the High Court in Glasgow. A steady stream of witnesses, a stream of women, and one recurring image: that of Webster fiddling with earphone buds

Claire Morris before the Black Widower took her life for insurance money. With her infectious smile, she was the life and soul of family parties.

The burnt out Daihatsu jeep which entombed Claire as her husband told would-be rescuers there was nobody else in the car.

The £208,000 insurance payout after the death of first wife Claire was gone in a matter of months. He bought cars and this yacht. He didn't bother paying off his mortgage.

A mortgage-free Felicity, working tax-free in the Emirates, happy and relaxed at a party with friends.

Till death do us part. A matter of hours after this happy walk up the aisle, on the first night of their honeymoon, Webster spiked his new wife's food with sedatives and Felicity spent the first 36 hours of their honeymoon comatose.

Malcolm Webster dons full Highland dress for his second wedding, this time on the other side of the world, to unsuspecting New Zealand nurse Felicity Drumm.

As family members mill outside the Auckland church, the happy couple pose for some amateur snaps.

The look of love, at least for Felicity.
For Webster, it was just another payday.

Felicity's parents pose happily behind their daughter, oblivious to the
fact that in a matter of months they would have to flee a fire in their
own home – a fire started by Webster to cover his own tracks.

Malcolm Webster fishing near his home in Oban on Scotland's west coast. He included this photo in a letter to his son Ned, unaware the net was closing in on him.

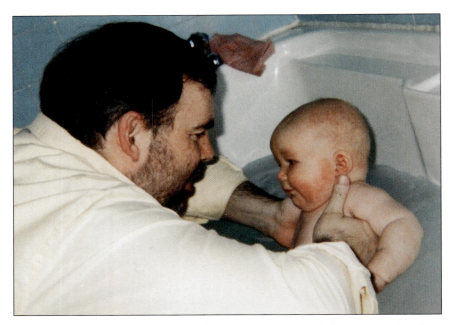

Webster bathes Ned, who suffered eczema as a baby. When daddy walked out of his life, Ned's skin condition cleared. The drugs Webster had been secretly feeding Felicity had been passed to Ned via breast-feeding, sparking the condition.

A proud mum. Life was finally as good as it gets for Felicity. A loving husband and a new baby son.

Felicity Drumm with sister Jane, post verdict. Jane's chance
conversation with a senior UK police officer sparked
a new UK probe into the Black Widower.

Webster shaved his head, eyebrows and body hair to fake
cancer in a bid to steal the estate of his third fiancee, Simone
Banarjee. He even pocked his arms with needle marks to
complete the ruse of medical treatment.

Simone Banarjee on her way to the High Court to confront the man who plotted her death in a bid to steal her fortune.
(© Press Association)

as he walked to the courtroom each day from his Glasgow hotel room.

The evidence amassed against him took so long to play out in front of the nine women and six men of the jury that it would require another book to reproduce it here. There are, however, some key points which Derek Ogg has highlighted as pivotal in the course of events at the court.

Webster was charged with the murder of his first wife Claire in a crash in Aberdeenshire in 1994. He was also charged with attempting to murder Felicity Drumm in New Zealand in 1999, and of attempting to bigamously marry Simone Banerjee to gain access to her estate. He was also accused of setting a number of fires to cover his tracks, and of stealing money.

However, it was all circumstantial, and Webster knew it. In the months leading up to the first day of the trial, he had remained silent in police interviews. The week after the *Sunday Mail* in Scotland ran the exclusive story of the probe, he told me, 'I am an innocent man. I did not kill my wife, and when the police find this out for themselves I will be only too happy to speak to you about it. I am helping the police to establish I am innocent. I am not hiding from anyone. The police know where I am.'

The pressure heaped on Webster by the publication of the world-exclusive story must have been immense. When the story broke, it spread around the world and even the ice-cold Webster must have felt the heat.

However, if he did, he didn't show it. He soon shook himself down and moved south, where he lived in his old family home, while various members of his family scattered the press outside and called on police to move them on.

Ironically, when the charges against Webster were first raised at an initial hearing in Scotland, Judge Lord Uist excused Webster from attending the next hearing as he had told the court he was 'short of funds' and had to report to police every day as part of his bail conditions.

Webster, throughout this episode, lived like a hermit. He was required to sign in at his local police station on a daily basis and had already surrendered his passport to Grampian Police.

The keen angler had certainly found himself in the net, but he wasn't landed just yet.

12

HELL HATH NO FURY

THE TRIAL OF MALCOLM WEBSTER COMMENCED ON THE morning of 1 February 2011. TV news that night showed a middle-aged portly man walking into court clutching a briefcase. He was bearded and bespectacled. He was listening to music on his beloved iPhone. Webster was a gadget and computer freak, and owned three PlayStations.

The courtroom was packed. It was a big case, the biggest most people in the room would ever experience. The atmosphere was heavy with expectation as the people in the public gallery stared at this everyman in the dock and tried to match him to the devilish indictment he had been summoned to answer.

In Scotland, the presumption of innocence means that very few people are remanded ahead of trial, even for capital offences. There would need to be a serious risk of flight or repeat offending for a prosecutor to successfully argue that an innocent man be locked up pending an outcome.

Thus, Webster's daily walk to and from the courthouse became a daily image on TV and caused Derek Ogg some angst as he ran the case.

Colleagues, even some on his own team, thought he should apply to have Webster remanded. Members of the public could not marry this image with the image of a cold-blooded killer.

As the weeks passed by and the evidence against him mounted, there was growing concern that he was still walking the streets, but Ogg waited until one week before the end of the trial to apply to have Webster remanded into custody pending an outcome. There was speculation at the time that Webster had been found with £1,000 in cash in his pockets and had been planning to flee the country. It seems even he knew, towards the end, that it was a hopeless case for him.

Cleverly, Ogg wanted people to see how calm Webster was. Only a sociopath could remain so calm while his world collapsed around him. At one point, Webster even waited at the revolving door to the courthouse, and gestured for a female prosecutor to go ahead of him. A gentleman to the end, it seemed.

At between 9 a.m. and 9.15 a.m. every day, Webster would arrive at court four. Most mornings, the courtroom was deserted, apart from one other person, the man trying to put him away for life, Derek Ogg.

Webster was always polite and civil to staff at the court, including Ogg. He would sit and read *The Telegraph* or his favourite car magazine, as Ogg went through the order of that day's witnesses just a few feet away.

From the vast jigsaw of evidence and witnesses listed at the trial, the pieces would fit together to reveal a picture of a monster, a man devoid of feeling who killed for money.

From the first witnesses, it became apparent this was no ordinary case. A series of world-renowned experts in forensics, crash-scene technology, detection and rate of fire burn would join ranks with a stream of women whose testimony was so heartfelt it left some in tears. When these victims gave their evidence, their voices seemed truer still as they rang out against a backdrop of utter silence. People were fascinated, captivated and appalled. Webster sat in the dock throughout, seemingly unfazed. His heart, however, must have been hammering out a different story.

The most compelling evidence in the trial, Ogg feels, came from the women directly affected by Webster.

Simone Banarjee was the first to give evidence against Webster and she held jurors spellbound and incredulous as she told the story of her life with him. She arrived at court wearing smart but casual clothes and walked purposefully into court four. She seemed to be a woman on a mission, but her heart was pumping. She appeared edgy and nervous at first, but settled into her evidence, and it soon became clear there would only be one outcome; that the jurors would see how much she had been duped, and how lucky she was to be standing before them.

Even Edgar Prais, Webster's own counsel in the case, told Simone, 'You are not just a lovely person, you are a loveable person.'

She may be loveable, but by her own admission she remains 'fragile' at times and said, 'I have tried to move on. Obviously I haven't moved on as well as I thought.'

Today, she is thanking her lucky stars for the intervention of the detectives from Strathclyde Police, but, at first, when they warned her the man she was about to marry was a danger to women, she refused to believe them.

Simone said she met Webster in 2004 in Oban and started a relationship with him in 2005.

In a key moment in the trial, Simone told the court that two CID officers handed her a letter alerting her about her fiancé's past. She said two detectives arrived at the Lorn & Islands District General Hospital in Oban in January 2008, with the letter, which had been signed by the assistant chief constable.

She said, 'It all seemed so unbelievable.'

Referring to the contents of the letter, Derek Ogg asked her, 'Did this seem to be the Malcolm Webster you knew?'

Simone, a quiet, intelligent woman, replied, 'No.'

She said, when she first met Webster in 2005, he had told her that his first wife Claire Morris had died in a car crash and that he had not remarried. The letter given to her by the CID officers revealed that Webster had married another woman, Felicity, in New Zealand and that they had a son.

Simone, in a state of shock, eventually confronted Webster as plain-clothes detectives waited outside in the garden, fearing for her safety. They had ordered her to tell them when she was going to tackle him so they could protect her.

She said, 'Initially he asked who told me. I said the police. He went white and very, very quiet and at that point I wished I wasn't in the room. I've never seen him like that before.'

By this point, Simone had known Webster for four years and had been in a relationship with him for two.

Ogg asked how long he remained like that and Simone replied, 'For five seconds maximum, then back to the Malcolm I knew.'

Mr Ogg asked, 'That was a place you didn't want to be?'

She said, 'No, I was terrified. He denied all the allegations it contained.'

In a touching courtroom tribute to Simone, Mr Ogg told her, 'One thing that maybe the defence and Crown can agree on, in this stage of your evidence, is you were in love with him because of who you believed him to be. The real Malcolm Webster is not someone you would fall in love with, Ms Banarjee.'

Tellingly, Simone replied, 'I have no idea who he is.'

In court, Simone was shown a picture of Webster with a shorn head – the very picture on the front cover of this book. Derek Ogg asked her, 'Does that shock you?'

She replied, 'It did, and it does to see it now.'

Ogg continued, 'Looking back on it now, do you think that there was a significant component of your involvement with Malcolm Webster which was to do with your sense of sympathy with the position he found himself in?'

Simone replied, 'Absolutely.'

Another telling piece of evidence which would stick in the minds of the jurors was her evidence that Webster had taken her to see his first wife Claire's grave and had also spoken about the car crash in which she died.

She said Mr Webster told her a motorcyclist came round a corner or the brow of a hill on the wrong side, he swerved off the road and the car caught fire. He had told her he could not get Claire out of the flaming car, that he himself had been trapped inside for a time and that the soles of his feet were burned before he managed to crawl out.

She added, 'I was told he was in intensive care for about a week after the accident.'

Mr Ogg told her, 'Mr Webster did not sustain any injury to his feet in the course of this crash. Are you certain he said this?'

She replied, 'I'm 100 per cent positive.'

Chillingly, Webster also told her he could hear his first wife screaming as the car burned, and that Claire was pregnant when she died.

In some of the most explosive evidence to be heard in the case, Simone also described how Webster told her he was suffering from chronic lymphatic leukaemia and had to go to the Royal Marsden Hospital in London for chemotherapy. By this time, he had completely shaved his head, eyebrows and body hair to complete the ruse. He would also tell her he was going away for treatment while he was secretly dating other women.

Simone told the court, 'I never met anyone who had been so unlucky in their life. To be bereaved and have a terminal illness.'

Mr Ogg said, 'It seems almost incredible.'

She replied, 'Yes it does.'

Ogg had successfully painted Webster as a philanderer and had taken the case beyond the legal 'no case to answer' stage. The jury needed to know why he was doing these things, and Simone's evidence in this regard was compelling.

She told the court she was in debt by the time they split up but had been independently wealthy before she met her fiancé. She believed Webster's money had come from the sale of a flat he said he had inherited from his uncle in Brighton.

Asked by Derek Ogg about his spending habits, she said they were 'out of control'.

She said, 'I believed him to be on a similar salary to myself. I don't know if he had money from another source, but I don't know if I could have spent the same amount myself without being beyond my means. He must have had some money from somewhere.'

As Ogg probed Simone on how she had coped with the realisation of the scale of Webster's deceit, her response echoed around the chamber: 'I'm OK if I don't think about it.'

That sentence alone must have driven a nail through any hopes the defence had of Webster talking his way around the evidence of the strong, brave woman who spoke so well and so truthfully. Simone Banarjee had just bared her soul to the world, and the jury, especially the nine women on it, could not miss the import of that last sentence.

Prosecutors felt it was important to include Simone's story on the charge sheet against Webster as she had come so close to tragedy and her story spoke volumes about the modus operandi of the man in their sights.

It was blatant. Junior counsel raised doubts over whether a charge of bigamy could be made to stick as he had never actually gone through with it. However, the moment Webster bought the ring and Simone the wedding dress, the charge of forming a bigamous relationship was a legitimate one. And it gave the Crown case the impetus it required to see the evidence over the finishing line.

It was almost an exact carbon copy of what had gone before – in the case of Claire and Felicity – and no jury could ignore it.

Simone Banarjee is wary of men, but happy not to be penniless or, worse still, dead at the hands of a psychopath she thought loved her. She was glad prosecutors included her story in the bigger picture, as she felt it gave jurors an up-to-date picture of how he operated.

Felicity Drumm knew she, too, would, one day, have to face her estranged husband in a courtroom, and the thought of it sent shivers down her spine. She finally came face to face with her tormentor in court four of the High Court on a cold February morning in Glasgow. Prosecutors had done their best to prepare her, even showing her a floor plan of the court which showed where he would be in relation to her position in the witness box. It only served to agitate her further when she saw how close to the dock she would have to stand as she gave her evidence.

'I had terrible butterflies about facing him in court but I actually found the whole experience very empowering and liberating,' Felicity recalled. 'I just had feelings of loathing and repulsion when I saw this pathetic blob sitting in the dock staring at the floor. He couldn't even make eye contact.

'Deep down I knew there was now nothing to be frightened of. It was my story and I didn't need to think twice about it.

'When I saw Malcolm sitting in the dock, with no care at all about what he'd done to me, the feeling of repulsion and loathing was actually quite liberating.'

Standing proud, with only the merest hint of nerves at the beginning of her testimony, Felicity stood her ground and gave evidence for seven full days in the witness box. At one point, she even asked defence QC Edgar Prais if she were the one on trial. But the jury, the prosecution and even Prais, the defence QC, loved her. She was telling the truth, her truth, the story of her horrible life with a man she had loved, and who had tried to kill her.

Why would she make this up? It was too embarrassing and macabre and no sane person would come to court and lie about some of the things that had happened to her. She had been conned, robbed, drugged and attempts had been made to murder her, and she saw none of it coming.

'He only made eye contact once and I could see he was completely detached from what was going on around him,' Felicity recalled. 'Sometimes I stared at him when I was having to give such personal information about our life together but he never stared me out.

'I honestly saw a quiet arrogance that he thought he was going to get away with it.'

Felicity Drumm has been left destitute by Webster. Prosecutors could not find a penny of her money, and throughout the long fight for justice she refused to divorce him, in order to protect any future victims. 'I have had to start my life from scratch again. Malcolm has always been like that with money; whenever he gets it, it's gone.'

It was evident to everyone listening that she was telling the truth about what had happened to her at the hands of a monster. Jurors began to steel themselves, while Webster, for most of the trial, seemed to have escaped into himself, like he wasn't completely there.

His defence QC, Edgar Prais, is usually a 'hail fellow well met'-type of silk who would breeze into court of a morning with a hello for all, but he was a different man throughout the Webster case. He spoke with his client each morning ahead of that day's evidence and would storm into court afterwards, brows lowered, not at all his usual form.

One morning, when his questioning of Felicity had been carried over from the night before, he took to his feet and, without so much as a hello, began immediately asking a question of her, picking up the thread of questioning from the previous day, as he walked to the lectern, his back turned to the Kiwi nurse.

Prais turned with a flourish to face her as he ended his question. It was a well-executed piece of early-morning court theatre.

Quietly, but firmly, Felicity Drumm began her response with

a measured, polite 'Good morning, Mr Prais,' which raised a chuckle from the public gallery and ended any further showboating from the by now exasperated QC.

She told him Webster had produced an 'Oscar-winning performance' after the car crash in New Zealand en route to the bank on 12 February 1999, to convince her he was having a heart attack.

She spoke with dignity about becoming unwell after eating food which was 'acrid' and 'bitter'. She said her husband broke down in tears when she mentioned it. He had been slowly poisoning her food, even when she was pregnant with their son. To this day, that is the one thing Felicity cannot fully comprehend, how Webster could have placed his own son's life in danger by drugging her.

She told the court, 'I had a few episodes following finding out I was pregnant. I was eating food. It was acrid and bitter. Quite disgusting. I can remember as far back as Saudi, not feeling right.

'If I continued to eat, I was feeling drunk. I would be staggering and needed assistance to walk. It was always at a weekend, always at home and always when Malcolm had prepared the food.'

She told jurors she asked Webster if he was putting something in her food and that he had broken down in tears. 'He became tearful and suggested that our marriage was in trouble if I would ever consider such a thought, and I felt guilty.

'I couldn't understand why it only happened in those circumstances. It never happened when I prepared the meal.

'I suppose it didn't make sense. We were happily married. Although I had a suspicion it didn't add up. We were in love. He would always insist I ate it all because I was pregnant and needed to maintain my nutrition.'

Felicity also spoke of confronting her husband after the car crash and said, 'It was quite clear his intention had been to kill me. He said I would have died happy. I had never been happier.

He had given me love, marriage and a child. In other words, I should be grateful.

'I felt sick and I felt repulsed by him. I had intended to spend the rest of my life with him.'

She then discovered Webster had insured her life for NZ$1.9 million, about £940,000.

Felicity said she was 'bewildered' by the fire at her parents' home in Auckland, when she and Webster were staying there, while trying to finalise the sale of the six-bedroom villa in Auckland she believed they had both set their hearts on. There was only one problem: Webster had no money.

It was during 'protracted' house negotiations that the fire broke out in the early hours of the morning.

She recalled, 'There was a very loud noise, an explosive noise or something which seemed very close. It seemed like it was coming from the living room.'

She told the court she had earlier seen Webster going into the living room after he got out of bed to go to the bathroom. She 'grabbed' her baby from his cot and alerted her parents, all of whom managed to escape.

She said she was 'totally bewildered. I couldn't believe that yet again something like this would happen to us. It seemed extraordinary that we'd had such a series of events. It didn't occur to me that anyone would purposefully destroy their home or possessions.'

What was not said in court was that, on the night in question, Webster had got up in the early hours and was missing for around ten minutes. Felicity was half-awake. Where she lay in bed, the bathroom was on the opposite side of the wall next to her side of the bed.

When Webster returned to bed, she asked him where he had been, and he said the bathroom.

She told police in her statement she knew this to be untrue, but in her half-waking state didn't have the energy to argue with him.

When she heard the explosive crack ten minutes later, she knew something was wrong, even though Webster tried to pacify her for a few minutes before getting out of bed once again to check. Police believe he was buying time so the fire would take hold.

He then returned to the bedroom and raised the alarm. A chair in the living room was on fire. The crack Felicity heard was the sound of a painting on the wall falling to the floor. The fire had crawled up the wall, behind the painting and burned through the string holding it in place. The loud crack had been the glass exploding as it hit the floor.

When the local fire chief turned up to assess the damage and cause, Webster said a remarkable thing. He blamed Felicity's nail varnish remover, which he said must have got on to the arm of the chair and spontaneously combusted.

The fire chief told Webster he had never heard of such a thing in his career. Webster replied that he had often set fires with varnish remover as a child in the Scouts. So forceful was he in this that the fire chief stopped debating it with him.

Most of Felicity's family were also flown to Glasgow from Auckland to give evidence. They all did so calmly and without preamble. One of the most memorable witnesses was Felicity's father Brian Drumm, a tell-it-like-it-is man and former high school principal, whose testimony the jury wholeheartedly believed.

Mr Drumm, now 82, said he discovered the couple's joint bank account had been emptied. He had turned detective after being tipped off by the family lawyer about money being taken from his daughter's bank account. Takapuna, where the family lived, was a small tight-knit community and Mr Drumm a well-respected figure within it.

He said, 'I made the deduction for myself.'

Mr Drumm alerted his daughter by phone, and most probably saved her life, rousing her from a drug-induced sleep just in time to see Webster pushing their son away from their car in a dark forest.

At home, they had discovered flammable materials in the boot, which prompted them to search through Webster's things. They looked in his briefcase and a box of his possessions, and found the key to a private mail box. They then found a bank statement that showed Webster was taking money from Felicity's bank account and sending it to his own account in Aberdeen, Scotland.

He also said that they came across a number of credit card bills which showed that Webster was in serious debt.

Mr Drumm said he then got a court injunction to prevent Webster approaching their family home.

Asked what the impact had been on his family, he replied, 'Dramatic.'

He also spoke of the night their home caught fire. 'We were raised by shouting from upstairs. There was shouting coming from Felicity and Malcolm that there was a fire.

'I ran upstairs and saw a chair on fire, ran back downstairs and filled a bucket up. I took it upstairs and threw it on the wall.'

Mr Drumm continued to run up and down the stairs, while Mr Webster filled a kettle with the toilet flush.

He said Webster told him, 'We'll laugh about this later.'

Felicity's mother Margaret was also called as a witness, and she was so overcome with the emotion of it all she had to ask to take a break while she was giving her evidence. Shortly after resuming her testimony, she hit Webster with an unbelievably beautiful and dignified parting shot, as only a mother who truly, unconditionally loves her daughter could do in a courtroom filled with strangers: 'If I may say so, Malcolm Webster had so much and he threw it all away.'

Jurors also heard from the elderly mother of his first victim, Claire Morris. Mrs Morris, now 85, who lives in Kent, was too frail to give her evidence in person at the court. The enormity of the case has taken its toll, but she is a strong woman who wanted justice for Claire, and her 18-page police statement was read to the jury. In her statement, Mrs Morris said Claire told her she and Webster had been involved in a smash where their car rolled over, one month before the fatal crash that left her dead in 1994.

And the witnesses just kept on coming, each painting a picture of a master of manipulation and deceit, as well as a cold detached man behind that charming façade.

Janet Davis, an old friend of Webster's, told jurors how he enjoyed the trappings of wealth and she recalled that he had told her he had been banned from Claire's funeral.

'He said Claire's mother was deeply upset and blamed Malcolm,' she said. 'He was not going to be allowed to attend the funeral, but there was going to be a memorial service for Claire.

'I didn't think it would be appropriate for me to go if Malcolm wasn't going to be there.'

Derek Ogg asked her, 'His mother-in-law had banned him?'

She replied, 'Because he was driving. Yes.'

Ogg then asked if she would be surprised to learn that Webster was not only at the service but, in fact, had 'arranged every detail of it'.

She answered, 'Yes.'

One piece of evidence uncovered by the Crown was that he got the date of his wife's death wrong in a letter he sent to one of her school friends.

Webster went to Saudi Arabia shortly after Claire's death and wrote to Susan Dolby, one of Claire's old school pals, on 3 April 1995. In it, he wrote, 'Life over here remains the same. I find that I miss Claire more each week. Maybe that is because I am away or that 26th May is getting nearer, I really don't know.'

In fact, Claire's death was on 27 May, or overnight into the 28th. The accident happened shortly before midnight.

Webster declined to be godparent to Susan's child, saying he had lost his faith in God and adding, 'I miss Claire so much I don't think I'd be very good at anything at the moment.'

143

Another friend of Claire's, Susan Campbell, said Webster had four cans of petrol in the boot of his car in the weeks before the fatal crash. She warned her friend Claire that carrying the petrol was dangerous and that her husband should know better.

Susan, a lecturer, said there was an overwhelming smell of petrol in Webster's Jeep one to two weeks before the fatal crash.

Susan's own husband had died in a car crash in 1988. She said, 'I asked Claire if there was something wrong with the car. She said there wasn't, there was fuel in the back of the car.

'It was so bad that I suggested that we open all the windows.'

She was asked by Ogg, 'Had you ever smelled that before in the car when you were in it?'

She replied, 'No. She said Malcolm used to carry the cans of petrol because he was afraid they would break down on the road.'

She also repeatedly tried to contact Webster after the fatal crash because she knew what it was like to lose someone in that way.

They met in a restaurant in Aberdeen, where they talked about the crash.

'I have very little recollection of that night,' she said. 'I went home and phoned my mother and cried and said, "He's moved on already. I still can't get over my husband. I find that very strange."'

Contained within the evidence against Webster was the quite remarkable story of Geraldine Oakley. Headlines of the day she gave her evidence speak of the woman who slept with Webster on the first anniversary of his wedding to Claire, but, when you look beyond the tabloid fodder of her evidence, there remains a quite remarkable series of events which, had they played out slightly differently, would have seen Webster behind bars years ago.

As Geraldine Oakley's relationship with Malcolm Webster

developed, she began to suspect he might have killed his wife. In fact, she was no longer sure if he was seeing her because he was attracted to her or because she was a computer manager at NHS Grampian.

Geraldine first met Webster in 1994, when she was working at NHS Grampian, as a computer manager in the same department where samples of Claire's tissues were stored.

They were friends prior to Claire's death. She was on holiday when it happened and said she became aware of it afterwards when she met Mr Webster, who was wearing a medical collar round his neck.

She said, 'He put his hands over mine and said there had been an accident and Claire had died. I told him to call me if he needed to talk.'

The court heard the pair went out for coffee and Webster invited Geraldine to his home near Oldmeldrum. She said Malcolm 'seemed keen to progress the relationship'.

On 3 September 1994 – the first anniversary of his wedding to Claire and only a few months after her death – Webster phoned her saying he did not want to be alone. She invited him to her home near Cruden Bay.

'He was entertaining. He made a joke and we ended up kissing. He ended up staying the night with me in my room.'

She said she soon became worried when Webster began to question her about whether a second autopsy was to be carried out on his young wife's body.

In a statement to police, she said, 'Malcolm was obsessed by this at the time and I considered speaking to consultant pathologist Dr James Grieve, but I never did.'

In fact, as we have seen, she was outside the office door of Dr Grieve on no less than three occasions, but couldn't bring herself to knock. Had she done so, Grieve would still have had access to retained blood samples taken from Claire's body, and would have tested for drugs. And that would have been the undoing of Webster.

Ogg asked, 'What was your conversation going to be about?'

Geraldine said, 'I thought that Malcolm might have killed his wife.'

Cross-examining, defence QC Edgar Prais quickly pounced on Geraldine's evidence, realising that, for the nine women of the jury at least, it was highly damaging to his client. He asked her, 'Are you telling us you had these views about a man who could be a murderer, and yet you were going to bed with him?'

She replied, 'It does seem a bit strange, but when you're in the middle of it you're thinking it can't quite be true when you're with someone who is charming and lovely.'

Even Webster's twin sister was called. Caroline Walters said her brother had told her he had lost all his money, after investing offshore in the Cayman Islands.

She said she told her brother he must have been 'one of the unluckiest people in the world' after Webster told her about a fire at the home of his second wife Felicity Drumm's parents in Auckland.

Incredibly, he also lied to his twin sister about having leukaemia, and said that on one occasion he turned up at her home in the south of England wearing a hat. When he took it off, his head was shaved and so were his eyebrows.

He kept up the deception until January 2008 when he finally confessed it had been a lie.

She also told how Webster had bought a share in a yacht with Simone Banarjee and that she thought they were trying for a child.

Mrs Walters added, 'Simone said, "He's not a murderer. We have been on the yacht many times. If he wanted to finish me off, he had plenty of opportunity."'

Ogg then asked if she knew Mr Webster had become engaged to Simone and she said, 'No. I knew he was very, very fond of her. I just assumed, having had two marriages, he wouldn't necessarily marry again. I knew Simone wanted a baby and I know they were trying for a baby.'

Ogg said, 'You knew he was still married to Felicity Drumm?'

Mrs Walters replied, 'I had an inkling that Simone might not know. I'd hoped that Malcolm would have told her.'

In another chilling insight into Webster's character, the court even heard about the funeral where Webster played the grieving husband, according to prosecutors. They claimed sociopath Webster was simply mimicking the emotions he thought he should be displaying at the time. He had spent months planning the crash which had brought them all to a quiet, rural cemetery to say goodbye to a loving, caring daughter and wife.

In fact, they said, her new husband had begun plotting how to profit from her death from the moment they met, while at the same time slipping her doses of the powerful sedative Temazepam. It was only later that friends and neighbours remarked on how drowsy she had become.

Claire's brother Peter said, 'It causes me great pain to think that she experienced all the joys and angst of first love and yet it was all a farce. It was a false love, just a ploy by a psychopath.'

At the time, nobody in the family thought for one moment that what had happened to Claire had been anything other than a tragic accident. When police finally did reopen the investigation into whether Claire had been killed by her husband, according to Peter, it was like an old wound being reopened.

Peter, who sat through the entire case, at first could not believe that cops were right about Webster. 'Even sat in court, I still had niggling doubts, and thought maybe the police had got it wrong. Malcolm was so convincing – sometimes I felt angry at him but other times I felt sympathy.'

However, as Peter and his wife Christine listened to the sorry saga unfold, there could be no doubt. He began to remember back, 13 years earlier, to some of the scenes he himself had witnessed. The roles Webster had played out so perfectly, loving husband, grieving partner. Naturally, he felt very angry.

He added, 'I had to sit through gruesome evidence, hearing

details of Claire's injuries. It was deeply upsetting but I felt I had to be there to finally know the truth about how my sister died.'

These witnesses had given an insight into the nature of the man. Their evidence built up a clear and damning picture of his character, no matter how tightly he tried to control his image to those around him, and showed Webster to be a manipulative and deceitful man.

The evidence presented by expert scientific, technical and financial witnesses, the prosecution believed, would prove he was also a murderer.

13

RETURN TO THE SCENE
OF THE CRIME

SOME OF THE MOST VITAL EVIDENCE AT THE TRIAL OF Malcolm Webster came from the statements from the past. Statements that were believed lost forever, forgotten about, then rediscovered in a dusty old police headquarters drawer.

Bus driver Kevin Shearer's evidence is remarkable for two reasons; he sadly died the week before he was due to take the witness stand, and, had it not been for an office clear-out at Grampian Police HQ in Aberdeen, his crucial statement to police, given at the time of the 'accident' which killed Claire Webster in 1994, would never have come to light.

Chief Inspector Phil Chapman, the man in charge of the massive cold-case police inquiry, had a problem. He could not find the original statements taken at the time of the crash in 1994. Junior officers had spent months searching the HQ for the paperwork but it was nowhere to be found.

They assumed the originals had been binned when computerisation was introduced to the force in the mid-'90s and thought nothing more of it. There was nothing anyone could do, but it was a huge blow to the prosecution team.

Then, shortly before the worldwide probe would be taken to court, prosecuting QC Derek Ogg, frustrated at not being able to get his hands on the original paperwork, received a telephone call from Chapman.

A junior staff member had been clearing an outer office, less than six feet from where Chapman sat throughout the probe, and walked into his office to ask if he needed 'the Webster crash statements'.

Assuming the officer meant the updated, more recent paperwork, Chapman, busy co-ordinating efforts to snare Webster, replied he had all he needed without looking up.

Then, when he did glance up, he caught sight of a dusty old folder, saw the officer blow dust off the top of it, and punched the air in delight.

The folder contained the original statements. They had been sitting less than six feet away from Chapman, in a forgotten desk drawer, for all those years. That paperwork contained the truth of what happened the night Claire Morris died, and their eventual discovery was the fillip Chapman and the rest of his hard-working team needed. It was a huge and welcome break for the worldwide probe into Malcolm Webster. Contained within the crackly papers was the evidence of Webster's actions and words on that night in 1994, which they used to devastating effect against him during the trial.

Within those typed-up reports of the evening in question was the truth. They now had a list of people who were on the scene, witnesses who had stopped and the position of the car as well as medical reports and all the usual forms that go along with a fatal road traffic accident.

More importantly, they also had reports of what Webster had said, how he had acted, what he had claimed had happened. They were a Godsend, and prosecutors believe without them they might have struggled to prove Webster had lied.

Police believed there was a reason bus driver Mr Shearer could not see flames or smoke as he arrived on the scene that night. Nor could he see anyone else inside the jeep. They believed Webster planned to push the jeep over the ravine then watch it, or make it, burst into flames, and, when he saw this vital witness approach, he had taken time to cover Claire with a blanket.

The bus driver's journey to collect some drunken lawyers had interrupted him. By the time Mr Shearer looked inside the jeep, Webster had already covered Claire with some kind of blanket to avoid detection, and was telling him repeatedly there was nobody inside. As we have seen, when they had set off on their midnight errand, he had thrown a blanket and a pillow into the car, later claiming Claire often slept through car journeys.

Claire Morris was alive when the flames took hold. She was breathing in smoke, according to the pathologist's report. So she was therefore alive when Mr Shearer came upon the crash.

Webster, not expecting to be disturbed so quickly at the scene, had to improvise to achieve his horrible aim. He had planned that Claire's body would be found in the burned-out wreckage at the bottom of the ravine. He would be able to say he swerved to avoid the biker and jumped clear of the jeep before it went over the edge, and was therefore unable to save his beloved wife.

The witnesses complicated this, and Webster had to think on his feet. He maintained that there was nobody inside the car when Mr Shearer found him on his hands and knees on the verge, seemingly dazed and confused.

Prosecutors believe that, when Shearer went off to summon help at a local farm, and before other witnesses arrived on the scene, Webster set the fire in the engine compartment of the jeep.

As he did so, he knew his wife was incapacitated, drugged, inside that very vehicle. That was the case led by the prosecution.

Prosecutor Derek Ogg said, 'The bus driver's evidence was excellent in so many ways, and it was tragic that he died before the case opened. His statement from the time gave us such an excellent overview of the scene. It told us there was no fire immediately after the crash; it told us that Claire at that time was not plainly visible in the passenger seat of the car.

'I think he wanted to drive or push the car over and into the ravine, so that he could tell the police he jumped clear and had no chance to save his wife. He must have been stunned to find that quiet country road so busy on that night. As a result he had to change his plan. That helped us, even all those years later, pick apart what he said at the time and prove that it could not have happened how he said it happened.

'The scientific examination of how he said it happened could not have been clearer, it was simply not possible that it happened the way he said it had.'

It was vital to show jurors that Webster's version of events on the night his wife Claire died was not physically possible. Planting the image in their minds of the actual scene in Aberdeenshire where Claire had died could only assist this.

Derek Ogg believed it was so important, in fact, that a visit was arranged. A Daihatsu Sportrak jeep was to be purchased and placed where Webster's original vehicle had come to rest on the quiet country road.

However, actually achieving the reconstruction proved more problematic than first thought. The investigating team, having had three of the jeeps at one point, had sold them on. Now they were on the hunt for another, and Ogg had even considered buying one out of his own pocket, so keen was he to show the jury the exact scene and position of the car on the fateful night. Fortunately, at the last minute officers from Grampian had found an exact match and bought it for £900.

Ogg has always maintained that Webster planned to roll the car over a steep ravine where it would then catch fire. Where it actually burst into flames is perpendicular to the roadside. He believes that, by the time witnesses spotted Webster on his hands and knees by the side of the road, it was too late to fulfil his plan and he improvised on the spot, telling those who had stopped to help that his drugged wife was inside the car only when he knew it was too late to rescue her from the flames.

One witness had actually looked in the jeep through the driver's side, and was able to see the pedals. However, he failed to see Claire Morris's body. Prosecutors believe that proved there was no smoke or fire on impact.

It would have been far easier had Webster been able to explain his jumping from the vehicle as it went over the ravine than to explain why he got out of the jeep yet his wife did not. He had not anticipated how busy the quiet country road would be that night.

As it turned out, back at the time of the crash, a rudimentary examination of the scene – and perhaps Webster's well-connected father, a senior Met Police chief – meant that these questions were never truly explored at the time. Ogg and the new Grampian inquiry team made no such mistakes when they revisited what they now believed to be a crime scene.

Jurors were shown the pictures of Claire Morris's charred and mangled body. They were too graphic to show to the public gallery. Not only was Webster able to do that to another human being, but he did it with witnesses around and without so much as a glance back after he had set the fire. He was too busy pretending to be dazed and confused. And he would go on to attempt it again, the Crown contested.

On the morning of 22 February 2011, some 17 years later, Webster would once again stand near the spot where he killed his first wife, his arms folded, and wearing sunglasses to protect his eyes from the low sun of a February morning, which was illuminating the woodland scene perfectly.

He was accompanied by a judge and the nine women and six men of the jury who would determine his fate. A Daihatsu Sportrak was lowered by crane to the exact position where it had been all those years ago.

The jurors spent 15 minutes appraising the scene, some even

ventured off road and down into the wood to see the ravine. All the while, Webster stood back, at the side of the road, his arms still folded, refusing to get too close. One can only imagine the thoughts racing through his mind at that time. Almost two decades later, here he was being held to account by his peers for his actions, being made to stand there and watch them pick apart his scheme. There are no sunglasses dark enough to mask that.

Webster's car lay perpendicular to the road; it was not a correct position for a car that had come off road after an accident, and at speed. Various experts were called in to testify to this assertion.

TRL – the company that had restaged the car crash in Paris's Alma Tunnel that had claimed the life of HRH Princess Diana – gave damning evidence against Webster's version of events. Science was being used to probe the past, and it shone a light into the darkness of Webster's scheme.

Stephen Jowitt, of TRL, was adamant that Webster had staged the crash. Their scientific evidence proved that Webster was lying.

A spokesman for the company said, 'In 2010, TRL was asked to assist Grampian Police on a cold-case basis to see whether the physical evidence available from the crash site corresponded to the version of events given by Mr Webster, or whether the incident was, in fact, a staged event, to cover up a murder committed to obtain money from a life insurance policy.

'TRL found that the available facts did not fit the accepted version, and decided that a more robust analysis was required. Using a 3D Laser Scanning System, as deployed when investigating the crash that killed Diana, Princess of Wales, TRL consultant James Manning mapped out the accident site, comprising the road and the wooded slope into which the car was driven.

'Using this three-dimensional platform as a basis, a model of the vehicle was driven off the road in avoidance, testing the account given by Mr Webster.

'The results revealed there was simply no match, as the car went straight past the point where the plans and photographs depicted an impact with a fallen tree.

'Two more situations were remodelled, based on the vehicle being steered intentionally into the woods at a low speed. Dramatically, the resulting impacts were consistent with the physical evidence.'

Stephen Jowitt's evidence was explosive. Science had proved what eyewitnesses at the time could not; that this was a staged event designed to kill for money.

Mr Jowitt told the court there was nothing to physically prevent Claire getting out of the car, if conscious. He said the car could also have been steered at slow speed. He had examined photos and statements given by Mr Webster and other witnesses, police and fire reports. He had also visited the scene for a report.

In his conclusion, he stated, 'It is highly likely that the vehicle was steered down the slope into the wooded area from a relatively low speed. Accordingly, the physical evidence fits entirely with the contention this was a staged event.

'It is highly unlikely that the vehicle entered the wooded area as the result of a high-speed veer. That is to say that this physical evidence does not support any interpretation of the version of events given by Mr Webster.'

Most damningly, he added, 'It is highly unlikely that the vehicle caught fire as a consequence of any impact damage generated in the incident.

'If this was an impact-related fire, the initiation of combustion would have been evident to an outside observer immediately after the impact. Accordingly, it is my opinion that the fire was deliberately set.'

The jury was even shown a series of animated simulations modelling both Mr Webster's version of events and staged crashes.

Mr Jowitt said, 'Unlike Mr Webster's version, a staged event could have produced all the physical effects documented after the event.'

Forensic fire investigator Andrew Wade said the blaze almost certainly started in the engine compartment of Webster's car and there was strong support for considering it deliberate.

'Never mind a book, this story has all the hallmarks of a Hollywood movie,' he told me.

He highlighted the time it took the fire to start, petrol canisters in the car and inactivity of the passenger Claire. In his report, Mr Wade said, in his opinion, if the fire had been caused by an electrical fault, it would not have taken so long for it to break out.

He concluded, 'This provides strong support for considering this to be a deliberate fire. By process of elimination, this seems the most probable cause, having examined all the possibilities.'

He said Webster's Daihatsu was angled down a bank so the flames would have spread up from the engine compartment into the passenger compartment. Claire's body appeared not to have moved from her reclined position in the passenger seat.

Mr Wade said, 'She appears to have been unaware of the fire.'

Dr Hugh Barron, a recognised expert in road traffic accidents, was too ill to give his evidence in person, and sadly passed away in April 2012. Instead, Judge Lord Bannatyne, advocate depute Derek Ogg QC and Webster's barrister Edgar Prais QC assembled in the courtroom, while Dr Barron answered questions from a police station in Aberdeen. The questioning was recorded and then played to the jury.

Lord Bannatyne had explained to the jury that it 'was decided this was the best way' to hear Dr Barron's evidence.

Dr Barron, 67, an engineering professor at the University of Aberdeen, compiled a report on the crash. He said he often worked with Grampian Police's road traffic investigation team.

His investigation seemed a simple one. Had Webster's car travelled off the road in a straight line or in an arc shape?

He also tried to work out what speed it was travelling at before it stopped, saying that, depending on factors such as the weight of the car and the friction between the vehicle and the road surface, it could have been travelling at between 17 mph and 24 mph, assuming full braking had been applied. Dr Barron thought it likely the car crashed at under 20 mph.

In his conclusion, Dr Barron said, 'It is most probable that to end up in its final position the Daihatsu would have to be driven off the road in a straight line at speeds of less than 20 mph.'

Dr Barron also gave his findings to a company which produced animations, using geometry and physics, of what would have happened to the Daihatsu at 25 mph and at 20 mph. He said that this showed it was not possible for the accident to have happened the way Mr Webster told police it had. It was damning evidence, and from a scientist with no axe to grind.

Police forensic officer Eric Jensen examined the burned-out wreck after the crash in 1994. He found the blaze was most likely to have started in the engine compartment of Webster's Daihatsu, possibly by a spark caused by a collision. This was backed by the Crown Office at the time. Mr Jensen, now retired, said, 'I don't say there was no evidence of foul play, just that my examination didn't reveal anything.

'The idea of somebody crashing a car and being able to set fire to it, deliberately under the bonnet, in the time he had – the guy is either a genius or he is extremely lucky.'

But Webster's luck had run out, and Ogg and his team were not finished yet.

Retired paramedic Robert Gallon said he and a colleague were called to the crash in the early hours of 28 May 1994. He said that, when they arrived, the car was still ablaze and Mr Webster was standing beside the fire engine.

When asked how Webster appeared, he replied, 'Slightly confused. He said he was OK. He asked us on two or three occasions how his wife was. I felt I was not in a position to say his wife had died.'

He recalled Webster's hair, eyebrows and clothing were not singed.

Webster had been examined in Aberdeen Royal Infirmary after the crash. Dr John Hiscox, a consultant in emergency medicine, said Mr Webster's pulse was 72 beats per minute, which the doctor described as normal. His blood pressure was also absolutely normal.

Police Inspector Ian Murray was one of the first people at the scene of the crash. He remembered Webster had not called out to officers to save his wife. Insp. Murray said the car was 'completely ablaze' when he arrived and there were no signs of movement from the burning car. There were no difficulties or obstacles that prevented him from taking Claire's body from the wreckage. The door was not obstructed on her side.

Witness Elizabeth Smith, a passer-by, wept as she told of the moment she saw the car burst into flames, after stopping at the scene.

She said, 'It was horrific, when I saw the jeep in flames and the woman lying in the seat.'

Retired Detective Sergeant Diane Taylor said Webster twice told her that there was no one in the car when they arrived at the scene. She said she later saw the outline of a body in the car lit up by flames.

The former officer was on her way home from having dinner with friends when she came across a jeep off the road and saw the accused on his hands and knees near it. The car engine was on fire and the jeep was filled with thick black smoke.

Mrs Taylor said she led Webster, who she described as conscious and lucid, to what she thought was a safe distance from the vehicle.

She said, 'I believed that man, saying there was no one in the vehicle.'

Mrs Taylor then recalled seeing someone being burned in the car. 'I was conscious of being told there was no one in the car and then seeing the horrendous sight I did afterwards,' she said. 'I feel terrible that I believed him and didn't open the car. When I saw what I saw afterwards I wish I had.'

Chillingly, when Mrs Taylor asked him where his wife was, Webster told her she was at home in bed.

Sergeant Colin Reid took a witness statement from Webster in Aberdeen Royal Infirmary after the crash on 28 May 1994. He said Webster told him the couple had set off after watching television. Sgt Reid said Webster claimed he made food, and he and his wife had watched the TV series *London's Burning*.

Webster told the officer they set off from the couple's home in Oldmeldrum, Aberdeenshire, to go to Royal Aberdeen Children's Hospital with documents which had to be delivered there that morning. He said he and his wife left their home and that in the boot of the Daihatsu Sportrak were three cans of petrol, two of which were almost full.

Sgt Reid said Webster told him that a motorcyclist had come towards the couple on the wrong side of the road, causing Webster to swerve off the road. Webster claimed that, if the motorcyclist had stopped, they could have got his wife out of the car.

Firefighter Derek McDonald also attended at the crash scene. In his evidence, he said he found no skid marks or debris, and minimal damage to the vehicle.

Mr McDonald said he had gone to the crash scene with cutting equipment, but was stood down and told to stand by.

Derek Ogg said, 'Did you hear the driver escaped unscathed?'

He replied, 'Yes.'

Ogg said, 'Putting these things together, the driver escaping unscathed, and the car did not have much damage, did you come to any conclusion?'

Mr McDonald replied, 'Definitely. I was extremely suspicious.'

Firefighter Albert Marr told the court he had attended the crash and was also told that Webster had gone off the road to avoid a speeding motorcyclist on the wrong side of the road. He said firefighters had searched woods near the blaze for the biker in case he was lying injured but did not find anything.

Another witness had spotted Webster a month before the crash in a field directly across from the scene of the crime. A local man, fearing for Webster's safety as there was a bull in the field, asked him what he was doing. Webster told him he was 'out for a walk'.

That man recognised Webster during the early days of the TV coverage of the trial and called police. He was quickly interviewed and summoned to appear.

Was this part of Webster's 'dry run' that Claire's mother had described in her police statement?

Curiously, a traffic policeman also told the court that, after going to senior officers to voice concerns about the crash in 1994, he was telephoned and told a line was to be drawn under the case.

David Allan, then a sergeant, said, 'I was told to move on and tell my colleagues to do so as well.'

Webster's father Alexander had been one of the most senior police officers in the United Kingdom, running the Metropolitan Police Service fraud squad and holding the rank of detective chief superintendent, just below the level of assistant commissioner and commander.

Sources close to the prosecution case and police inquiry made enquiries to establish whether Webster's father made any contact during the probe into the fatal car crash that night.

Certainly, experienced officers who smelled a rat were told to 'forget about it' and to this day those who remember the crash site regret that they did not push harder. One claimed, 'It was obvious we were dealing with someone connected.'

It is almost certainly the case that Webster's father helped him on many occasions. He paid for airline tickets to help his son evade capture by New Zealand Police and he may have used Foreign Office connections to smooth his son's exit from Abu Dhabi in the wake of the children's deaths in the hospital.

He was not averse to picking up the telephone to act in his son's best interests, and those involved in the review which began in 2006 and the subsequent court case considered whether he might have brought his considerable influence to bear. Could this influence have delayed justice for over 17 years?

14

EVEREST SCALED

THE SHEER VOLUME OF EVIDENCE SPANNED MANY AREAS of expertise, but Derek Ogg QC feels perhaps the single most important breakthrough in the case came from the 'sliver of liver', the discovery that relaunched the entire police investigation into Webster. It was a horrible phrase for the relatives of Claire Morris, as it referred to a tiny piece of her, stored since the 'accident' in 1994.

Dr James Grieve gave evidence to the High Court in Glasgow that Webster's first wife Claire's liver sample was tested in 2007. He found traces of a drug in her liver tissue. He said that the probability was 92.4 per cent that the substance found was Temazepam.

Dr Grieve told how he had used a new technique to check Claire's liver. It had never been done before, anywhere, and is described in more detail elsewhere in this book, but the lengths to which Grieve went serve to underline the severity of the case, and how seriously Grampian Police had taken it. The prosecution of Malcolm Webster's case by Grampian Police would stand or fall, depending upon the result.

Another vital witness, according to Ogg, was New Zealand police officer Glenn Gray. The Drumms believe that without him justice would never have been done. Felicity's sister Jane believes New Zealand Police 'should clone him'.

The court heard that Detective Gray first became involved in the case when Felicity went to police after realising that her husband had taken all the money from their account.

Derek Ogg asked the officer, 'When you saw her initially, did her complaint centre around missing funds from her bank account which pointed towards her husband being the culprit?'

He replied, 'Yes.'

Mr Ogg asked, 'Subsequently did she inform you of blackouts she had?'

He again replied, 'Yes.'

The detective then said he had contacted Interpol and the Grampian and Strathclyde police forces in connection with the case, and ordered an investigation into the fire at the home of Felicity's parents in Auckland two days before Felicity and Webster were involved in a car crash.

He concluded that the fire and another at the house the couple intended to buy were arson attacks.

Gray also arranged for drug testing to be carried out on a sample of Felicity's hair. It came back positive and proved what she had feared. Webster had drugged her throughout their relationship, even when she was pregnant with their baby.

The officer headed the investigation in New Zealand from February 1999 until November 2008. He was one of the first people Felicity Drumm thanked after her nightmare ended, a tenacious small-town cop who battled for years to persuade colleagues in the UK they had a dangerous predator in their midst.

Another key line of inquiry had been the financial aspect of Webster's crimes, and investigators throughout the case followed the money, the very thing that had allowed them to prosecute Webster in Scotland in the first place. There was so much of it, and the way Webster spent it left him open to suspicion.

He received a £208,000 insurance payout after the death of

his first wife. He failed to pay off his mortgage and blew nearly every penny within six months. Stunned cops discovered that at some points he was spending £3,000 a day. Chillingly, one of the first things he did on release from hospital after the crash was to cash in the insurance.

The detectives leading the inquiry had to attempt to pull together a financial picture of Webster going back almost two decades. There were masses of financial records and bank logs, some of which had been lost forever.

It also transpired that, at the same time as he was plotting murder, he was being chased by debt collectors.

Accountant Ann Condick told the court that Webster spent almost £200,000 of the insurance money he received after the death of his first wife within six months. She said that, in the month leading up to Claire Morris's death, Webster was in thousands of pounds of debt. 'It seemed to me he was living well beyond his means,' she said. 'When he was not able to take further credit from a card, he would take out another one or get a loan which put him further in debt.'

Webster was being pursued by debt collectors for credit card arrears of thousands of pounds, and he knew how to spend money. Prosecutors believe to this day that a large chunk of the £1 million-plus he gained through murder and arson is still out there somewhere, hidden away by a man whose love of possessions knew no bounds.

Investigators found no less than three American Express cards, all of which were in arrears, as well as over a dozen cards from various other lenders, each card taken out to pay off the debt accrued on the previous one; that vicious cycle of debt in which many people find themselves. However, not many of them would choose to break that cycle in the despicable way that Webster had done.

He also owed money on store cards from Harrods, John Lewis and Fraser's and was being chased up for these debts by collectors, having ignored the letters and telephone calls. His

Harrods store card was opened in December 1992 and the closing balance was £4,078.26 in debt. His credit limit at that time was £3,500, so he had already been spending what he didn't have and buying time to pay it off, hence the negative balances. The debt was written off in September 2000 and sold to a collection agency. On his Fraser's card alone the credit limit was £2,750, but Webster managed to rack up £3,103.89 of debt. That amount was also sold on to a debt-collection agency. When John Lewis eventually closed off his card, it was in arrears of £848.88.

He used the cards to buy music, software and photographic equipment. He also liked to frequent antiques shops and had a keen interest in antique clocks. Prosecutors keen to trace his money spoke to many local dealers both in Scotland and abroad, as well as a number of web-based firms who all sold items, such as paintings, clocks and watches, to Webster. He liked chatting to the store owners and discussing paintings and watches. As one said, 'He enjoyed the whole experience. He would say, "Now how much for this piece?" and be told £10,000 and he would stroke his chin and reply, "And could we reach agreement at around £8,000, perhaps?"

'He always liked to let you know that he knew as much, if not more than you about the object you were discussing.'

There was a rather startling picture emerging. Webster needed money, fast, to repay the life he had been living. He had enjoyed it, but it had all been on credit, and his creditors were looking to be repaid.

None of this was examined at the time of Claire's death. It is shocking to think of that now, but at the time officers believed this was an accident, and had no way of knowing or deducing otherwise. Of course, they did not have the benefit of knowing about Webster's subsequent criminality, and they had no reason to suspect a newly married son of a cop with no criminal record.

When Claire died, Webster bought a Land Rover, a yacht, a

fancy watch and various other adornments that he felt suited his newfound wealth. He was finally the rich man he always believed he deserved to be.

The medical evidence presented also added to the damning picture being built up of a cold and calculating murderer.

The jury was told that Claire had visited her GP twice in the weeks before she died, complaining of fatigue. Dr Francis Howarth had taken blood tests, which came back normal.

Ogg then asked Dr Howarth, 'You did not do any toxicology tests to see if she was taking, abusing or being given drugs?'

He replied, 'I didn't test for that.'

When Dr Howarth was asked if he would have prescribed Temazepam for her, he replied, 'No.'

Webster himself visited his doctor in Aberdeen five times complaining of a back injury and was given a total of 191 Diazepam tablets.

Dr Jennifer Brownhill said Webster first visited her practice on February 1998 complaining of back pain after taking a printer out of the loft of his home, at a time when Felicity was constantly complaining of being fatigued and sleeping for long periods.

On this first consultation, he was prescribed 20 Diazepam tablets as a muscle relaxant and Brufen to deal with inflammation.

Webster's medical notes say that he returned the following week. He said he continued to have pain in his lower back especially in bed and was having difficulty sleeping. He was told to put ice on the affected area and was prescribed a further 21 Diazepam tablets and 60 Diclofenac tablets.

He went back to the GP practice again, this time complaining of a recurrence of his lower back pain after lifting heavy suitcases into a car. It now seems clear he was obtaining and storing tablets that could kill.

This time, Webster was given 60 Diclofenac tablets and 30

Diazepam. He returned to the doctor yet again, saying he was still having problems with back pain and was given 50 Diazepam tablets.

His final visit to the GP surgery was on 23 July 1998. Dr Brownhill said, 'There were further problems with low back pain after lifting a baby bath.'

On this occasion, Webster was given 60 Diazepam tablets and 84 Diclofenac tablets.

Mr Ogg said, 'So, between February and July 1998, Mr Webster was given 191 Diazepam tablets and he would legitimately have these in prescription bottles?'

Dr Brownhill said, 'Yes. That's correct.'

Webster also had free access to drugs while working at Aberdeen Royal Infirmary, when he was living with and married to first wife Claire.

Gina Andrew, a ward sister at Aberdeen Royal Infirmary, said there was no system for tracking drugs once they had been sent to the medication cupboard on the ward. She said drugs available included the sedatives Diazepam and Temazepam, and the epilepsy drug Epizyme.

Mr Ogg, ever keen to join the pieces of the jigsaw for the jury, asked Gina, 'If a nurse wanted to take Temazepam, Diazepam, Valium or Epizyme out of a cupboard on the ward, and then out of the ward, that could be accomplished with no trace of that having happened?'

She replied, 'That could have happened.'

Webster had worked in the same ward as Gina until around 1993 when he took up a role in the new computerised nursing department. She said that half of the ward where they worked was dedicated to haematology, and added that much of the work involved the testing for and treatment of leukaemia. Webster, therefore, would have been well aware of the symptoms of that disease.

Nurse Lesley Roberts, who had become good friends with Claire in the six months before she died, went to police after hearing rumours in 2006 about a crash involving Webster's second wife. She had never believed the crash that killed her friend was an accident. Her suspicions had been raised very soon after Claire's death when she spotted epilepsy medication in the house Claire shared with Webster, even though neither of them suffered from the condition.

After hearing rumours about Webster in 2006, she went into a police station in Anstruther to give a statement, convinced he had murdered Claire.

Ogg said, 'The suggestion is that his second wife had been poisoned and you linked that with the fact you have never been happy about the way Claire met her death and you went to the police to say look at it again.'

Lesley replied, 'Yes.'

So many witnesses, all voicing their doubts and concerns at the manner of Claire's death.

But there was more. One witness in particular gave jurors serious pause for thought.

Detective Constable Brian Moggach, a computer analyst with Grampian Police, had been brought into Operation Field – the name given to the investigation into Webster – in May 2008. He had been given computers that were connected to Webster, and, along with a colleague, he copied the information from the hard drives and then examined the copies. Among the information discovered – including ten deleted emails from Webster to Brenda Grant in the US, referring to his chemotherapy – rather chillingly, DC Moggach had found a report on Dr Harold Shipman.

Shipman, who killed at least 215 people over 23 years by giving them overdoses of Diamorphine, was jailed for life in 2000 for 15 counts of murder. He was found hanged in his cell at Wakefield Prison in January 2004.

The Shipman inquiry later concluded he was probably responsible for about 250 deaths.

Derek Ogg asked DC Moggach, 'Did you find the report on

the inquiry into the doctor who was convicted of murder, Dr Harold Shipman?'

The police officer replied, 'Yes.'

Ogg then asked, 'Was there a connection to the Shipman inquiry found in the address sector of the computer?'

Moggach replied, 'Yes, there was.'

On 3 May 2011, the prosecution case closed after 50 days of evidence. There had been a wealth of technical, scientific and financial evidence from experts and witnesses around the globe, but most damning of all was the heartfelt testimony of the women in his life who told their stories of love and betrayal. The jury heard tales of druggings, lies, deception and premeditated murder. Webster had been exposed as a serial philanderer, a man who had used his considerable charm and personality to manipulate women for his own ends. Now he was to take the stand in his own defence, could he do the same to the jury?

15

15 MINUTES OF INFAMY

WHEN WEBSTER TOOK THE STAND TO GIVE EVIDENCE IN HIS own defence, he did not look like a man fighting for his life. He seemed almost lacklustre in his responses. Whether this was a deliberate attempt to play down the seriousness of the charges or he had simply given up by this point is hard to tell.

Mr Prais asked, 'Did you stage the accident so that you could murder your wife?'

Webster replied, 'No, I did not.'

Mr Prais then asked, 'Did you take out insurance policies so that, having murdered your wife, you could reap your ill-gotten gains?'

Again, Webster said, 'No.'

Mr Prais asked of the New Zealand crash, 'Did you deliberately leave the road?'

He said, 'Yes, because I was on my way with Felicity, we were going to the bank and I knew that there were no funds there.'

He said he did not want to kill or hurt Felicity, and that he had not acted for 'ill-gotten gains' through life insurance.

Surprisingly, Mr Prais questioned Webster for just 15 minutes. In fact, he later confessed that 15 minutes was as long as he could hope to have with Webster before he changed his story, and confided to friends he was 'an awful man for changing his story'.

Naturally, prosecuting counsel Derek Ogg would not let him off so lightly.

When Ogg rose to cross-examine Webster, he described Claire's death as a 'cold-blooded, premeditated, carefully planned murder that went precisely according to plan'.

Webster replied, 'I'm telling you it was not a murder, it was a tragic accident.'

Ogg told Webster, 'All the facts in this case that have been painstakingly researched and spoken to become a blizzard that blows in one direction – you are as guilty as sin of murdering Claire.'

He replied, 'I didn't murder Claire. I was avoiding a motorcyclist, the lights of a motorcyclist, on my way back to the cottage. I swerved to the left, that's all I can remember of the situation. I know that I didn't hit the motorcyclist.'

Turning to the Auckland crash with Felicity, Ogg said there were similarities between the two crashes. He said, 'That's why you had to go to the other end of the world to carry it out, so that someone like me could not make the connection.

'It's the only safe place to murder a second wife, the other end of the world.'

Suggesting a motive, Ogg told Webster, 'The position in the bizarre world of Malcolm Webster includes the deliberate and callous targeting of women – your first wife, your second wife and Simone Banarjee – the grooming of them for your own vicious, greedy ends.

'It has nothing to do with love, but all to do with money. It's the most base motive for murder and that is what the evidence shows, is it not?'

Webster calmly replied, 'No, sir.'

Mr Ogg then said, 'You are a murderer and set out to murder your second wife.'

He replied, 'No, sir.'

Webster also told the court that he had never told Felicity she would have 'died happy', as she claimed when she accused him of trying to kill her.

Referring to the charge of attempted bigamy with Simone, Ogg told Webster, 'There was no record in the UK of you being married to Felicity Drumm.'

Webster replied, 'First of all, I wouldn't have married her. I was already married at the time.'

He also claimed that Oban, where he and Simone both lived and worked, was such a small place that she would eventually have found out he was married.

In his closing speech, Ogg labelled Webster a 'brilliant criminal genius' whose only flaw was 'he can't stop himself. For 17 years, it was the perfect murder. He got away with it for 17 years because he made it look like an accident.'

The prosecutor said that all the individual pieces of evidence against him came together to 'form a web, a mesh, a net that caught him so fast and so completely'.

He compared the circumstantial evidence to a 1,000-piece jigsaw with some of the pieces missing, and added, 'There are bits missing, but we can still see what it is meant to be.'

He said that both wives loved and trusted Webster, and he repaid that by killing the first, and robbing and attempting to murder the second.

He called the Black Widower a 'most cruel, practised deceiver' and said Webster 'would be one of the most notorious murderers of modern times'.

'This is someone who has sat down and carefully and calmly planned the destruction of a person who believed he loved her. Who could do such a thing?'

He said the accused had groomed and targeted all three of his victims.

He compared the car crashes involving Webster's two wives

and said, 'Luckily for Felicity Drumm along came the police right after the crash.

'The Crown view is that this was a deliberate attempt to destroy her life.'

He told the jury that Simone's evidence showed Webster claimed to her that he was dying from leukaemia. He added, 'This was psychological sadism. Can you imagine the mentality that does that? What does he get out of it? What kind of person does that? What's he thinking, watching her reaction, seeing her upset, seeing how brave she is being to him?'

He ended his address to the jury with the words: 'I submit that his reign of destruction is at an end.'

Edgar Prais QC said his client was not a murderer, but he adopted a peculiar tack with his address to jurors, one that reflected the seriousness of the offences Webster was facing.

'He is a liar, he is a thief, he is a philanderer,' he said. 'He is all those things.'

He said Webster fitted those categories 'shamefacedly but admittedly'.

Mr Prais pointed at Webster in the dock and told the jury, 'You would be right to conclude that a woman, any woman, would have to be nuts to give her heart or her money to that man.

'Equally, you should arrive at the conclusion on the evidence, however much of a rat bag he might have been, he is not a murderer or even an attempted murderer.'

He said there was no evidence led by the Crown to show that the Daihatsu Sportrak in which Claire died had been deliberately set on fire and said it was a case of 'compare the witnesses dot com' and 'compare the statements dot com'.

He said, 'You have got to be careful. You have got to look at things very, very carefully.

'This is not a case about property. This is not a case about pounds and pence or New Zealand dollars and cents.

'This is a case about life and death.

'You don't say Claire died such a God-awful death and somebody's got to pay for it.'

On 19 May 2011, the jury retired to reach a verdict. They returned in less than four hours: guilty on all counts.

The judge, Lord Bannatyne, thanked them and excused them from ever having to sit through jury duty again. They had become part of the fabric of a gargantuan trial, one that Ogg and his team had successfully whittled down to present to them in a clear and coherent way. They showed Malcolm Webster no mercy. On two different continents, the cheers went up.

16

'A CONSIDERABLE DANGER
TO WOMEN'

ON 5 JULY 2011, MALCOLM WEBSTER WAS BROUGHT TO
court to learn his fate.

On sentencing, Lord Bannatyne told him, 'You were
convicted by a jury of all the charges you faced on this lengthy
indictment. The most serious of these charges . . . being a
charge relating to the murder of your then wife, Claire Jennifer
Morris.

'The sentence which I impose on that charge is the one
prescribed by law, namely life imprisonment. I also have to
impose a punishment part. The murder of your then wife was
an appalling act and all right-minded people will be utterly
shocked by it.

'The murder of your wife was premeditated. It was carefully
planned and put into effect over a period of time. Over a
number of months you administered drugs to her. On the night
of her death, you again administered drugs to her, thus
rendering her unconscious.

'You then drove her to a site you had already identified.
There you faked a car accident. You then deliberately set the
vehicle on fire while knowing that your wife was unconscious
within the vehicle and wholly unable to save herself.

'This was a murder which could properly be described as cold-blooded, brutal and callous. This murder was the central part of a plan to obtain for yourself by fraud money from various bodies. Your motive for this murder was thus the utterly base one of financial gain.

'This was a murder of a wholly exceptional kind and of a type rarely seen in these courts. It is a crime for which you have shown no remorse and I am unable to identify any factors which mitigate at all this dreadful crime.

'When imposing a punishment part, the court is directed to have regard to the other offences on the indictment apart from the murder of which the accused has been convicted. You were convicted of a number of other crimes on this indictment. I would intend only to refer to the two most serious of these, namely the two further convictions for the attempted murder of Ms Drumm. Charge 3(2) again involves the administering of drugs to your victim over a period of time. Once more this was a cold-blooded crime. In addition, it involved the endangerment of Ms Drumm's unborn child.

'Charge 3(14) is a further staged road accident involving an attempt to murder Ms Drumm.

'Once more, these were the central planks in a carefully laid plan made by and put into effect by you in order to financially gain from the death of your then wife.

'Having regard to the circumstances of the murder, the nature and circumstances of all the other charges of which you were convicted on the indictment and the whole other facts and circumstances before me I impose a punishment part of 30 years backdated to 12 May 2011.

'I now turn to the other charges on the indictment. As regards charges 6 and 7, these were, in my view, both very nasty offences. In terms of charge 6, you in all real senses took the entire savings of Ms Drumm and left her destitute.

'As regards charge 7, your behaviour, though in no way as serious as in relation to the earlier charges involving Claire

Webster and Ms Drumm, must have been very distressing to Ms Banarjee. Accordingly, on charge 6, you will go to prison for four years and, on charge 7, you will go to prison for three years.

'Lastly, when imposing the punishment part, I am directed not to take into account the period of imprisonment necessary for the protection of the public and I have not done so.

'However, I have formed the clear view on the basis of the evidence led and such reports as are before me that you are a considerable danger to women and I would intend to so advise the appropriate authorities.'

It seemed Webster was in a world of his own throughout these statements. He had blocked off the speeches, the condemnation, and, while physically he was sitting in the dock, mentally he was somewhere else. There was no emotion, not there, in public. He kept that in check until he was taken below stairs, to a world he knew nothing about.

New Zealand Police Detective Glenn Gray, a dogged and modest officer whose tenacity ensured a successful outcome for the Drumms and everyone else affected by Webster's greedy spree in the United Kingdom, said the eventual guilty verdict was, for him, 'fantastic, really good, it has been a long time coming and it was a good sentence that will keep him out of harm's way until he is at least 80 years old, so I'm really, really happy with it.

'For me personally, it would be my career highlight, and it's just nice to know he's not going to be a problem to anyone, not when he gets out at the age of 80 or 82. I've spoken to Felicity and the family and they're of the same opinion as myself. I've known these people a long time now and it's been a long time coming for them, at huge personal cost to them emotionally and in terms of time, hanging in with the inquiry over the years and appearing in court.

'They know that nobody else is going to get hurt by this guy, so that's huge vindication for them.

'In 2006, 2007, the case gained momentum again in Scotland. His pattern of offending is what got him caught. He just offended against so many people, and so many things he did were based upon a lie. It was a huge stack of cards. He got away with it by having that English-gentleman persona. I spoke with him very briefly at the very beginning of the complaint by Felicity. He is just completely self-centred, self-absorbed. He was always able to answer things away.

'Everything was about Malcolm Webster and his own gain. If Webster is ever released again, he'll be a danger to the life of any woman he comes across. Psychologically, I've never seen anyone like him before in my time in the job. I've never seen anyone whose life was such a lie.'

Grampian Detective Chief Inspector Phil Chapman was the senior investigating officer in charge of the inquiry team of 25 detectives. They interviewed a thousand people, and six of the officers, including Chapman, spent a month in New Zealand investigating the Felicity Drumm case, as well as reinvestigating Claire's death. He knew he was dealing with a man who killed for money from a very early stage.

'His contempt for human life was to feed an insatiable appetite for the trappings of wealth. The first thing Webster did on getting out of hospital after murdering Claire was to go and claim on one of the insurance policies on her life.

'The vast majority of people we spoke to described him as charming. But when you remove the mask, what you reveal is an individual absolutely driven by money.'

DCI Chapman continued, 'Malcolm Webster's crimes were extensively planned and thought out.

'Claire's mum always held a belief that something else had happened and felt there was more to it. I think it was quite cathartic for her when we approached her to say we were looking into what happened to Claire. The family was very dignified and said they just wanted the truth.

'We spoke to Malcolm and detained him in relation to the

murder of Claire. He was very calm; he just said "no comment". He exercised his right not to speak and he was very much compliant, just as he had told the media that he would be. He has never been unruly and he allowed us to go about our business, never commenting, but that was his right. Malcolm cannot be anything but hugely arrogant. With most homicides, you find that they were spontaneous acts, very rarely do you have a premeditated homicide.

'In Malcolm's case, he considered, planned and executed a specific plan, which shows total contempt for human life. His absolute greed is ultimately what has undone him.

'Malcolm's motivation was money and his insatiable appetite for wealth.'

He said Webster was a 'charming individual', but under the veneer there was a 'chilling disposition'.

He added, 'I would like to thank and pay tribute to the dignity and courage shown by Betty and Peter Morris and her extended family during the course of our inquiry.

'In February 2008, I first met Claire's family and had to tell them that we believed Claire's death, 14 years earlier, was not a tragic accident, but a premeditated and planned murder, committed by her husband, the man to whom she had pledged her life.

'This was clearly a devastating revelation, which generated many questions and a range of traumatic emotions for them.

'I would also like to thank Felicity Drumm and her family, whose collective determination and resolve to bring Malcolm Webster to justice can only be commended.

'Indeed, it was the family's pursuit of Malcolm Webster which led us to reconsider the circumstances surrounding Claire's death.'

He added, 'He peddled his lies across different continents believing his chilling and callous crimes would go undetected. But he severely underestimated the determination and will of the many people whom he had deceived.

'It was only after a painstaking investigation into Malcolm Webster's life, taking us literally to the other side of the world, and using truly innovative technology and investigative techniques, that the true magnitude of his crimes became clear.'

Speaking about the vital sliver of liver breakthrough, DCI Chapman took time to pay tribute to the work of Dr Grieve: 'We were told it had never been done before. It's not something that's ever been tried before. We are talking a minute piece of tissue sample. You get one go at it and thereafter there's nothing left. You will find absolutely no trace of any previous forensic toxicological examination like they conducted. From their point of view, it was absolutely cutting edge. It's not the type of thing that has, in mainstream toxicology, ever been done because there's no real requirement for it.'

Mr Chapman, who has been a police officer for 20 years and led several high-profile murder investigations, said the liver test was a striking breakthrough for the team. 'That clearly was a significant development for us in that Felicity Drumm's position was always that she had been drugged and that various tests had been conducted which had detected the presence of Benzodiazepines in her body.'

He helped build the mass of evidence that piled up against Webster's door by the end of the case. He is proud of that, as are the dozens if not hundreds of investigators who played their parts in bringing Webster's campaign to an end.

Lindsey Miller, head of the Serious and Organised Crime Division (SOCD) at the Crown Office and Procurator Fiscal Service, said, 'This was a hugely complex case, involving hundreds of witnesses, productions and financial documentary evidence stretching over a 14-year period. A vast amount of painstaking work went into this investigation and prosecution.

'Webster was a calculating criminal who wove a web of lies and deceit around people who entered his life in good faith.

'I would like to commend the persistence and tenacity of all those who worked tirelessly to bring Webster to justice for these appalling crimes.'

Retired detective Charles Henry, who had helped protect Simone from Webster in Oban, said, 'He has been convicted of the premeditated murder of one woman and the attempted murder of another woman.

'The emotional damage that he has caused to some of the ladies who have been in his life is incalculable. Here were these women that thought they were in love with a totally charming, upfront, honest, sophisticated gentleman. But it turned out that he lied and cheated at every particular turn. Not only that, if things did not go his way, then they were at risk.'

However, none of them was ever frightened of him until police exposed his crimes. His secret weapon was not his looks, his wealth or his athletic prowess, but his charm.

Prosecutor Derek Ogg QC said, 'Everyone described him as "charming". He was charming and disarming.'

The Webster inquiry is estimated to have cost over £5 million, but how can you put a price on justice for so many people?

In the largest international investigation of its kind the force has dealt with, officers took witness statements from people in countries including New Zealand, Australia, Sierra Leone, America, France and Spain. The FBI was drafted in to take statements in the US.

Officers from Grampian Police travelled to New Zealand to interview witnesses in 2008, including Felicity Drumm and her family, and worked with the FBI and SOCA (Serious Organised Crime Agency) and police forces in England and Wales.

Prosecutors spent fortunes bringing witnesses to court, £55,000 to fly witnesses in from New Zealand alone. The total travel bill for the trial hit £97,000.

UK witnesses cost £20,323 for travel, £5,286 for lost earnings, £31,192 for subsistence and the trial cost the taxpayer £13,429 in expert witness fees alone.

Officers built up a 17-year profile of Webster and could tell what his wealth, or lack of it, was at any time. One thing is certain: Malcolm Webster is poorer today for that kind of dedication.

They may not understand him, but they got deep enough into his psyche, his way of operating, to catch him. Everyone connected to the case, directly or indirectly, has a theory on who he is, what he is and why he did what he did.

These range from a callous cold-hearted opportunist right through to that most dangerous animal on the criminal spectrum, a serial killer.

Many people, including some of those who spent years prosecuting the case, believe Webster is quite simply a serial killer who was caught early. A monster in the making.

It is little comfort to the family of Claire Morris that he was caught early. It was already too late for them.

Webster's heart must have sunk to his boots as he sat in the dock listening to the best his own QC could muster in a bid to sway the jury, as Prais called him a man like no other, a serial philanderer, a liar, a cheat.

We all know people who could tick all of those boxes, but that would hardly make them a serial killer in the making.

It was the extent to which Webster would carry on the deception, the extent to which he planned his crimes, and the total lack of emotion displayed as he did so. A love rat may have sleepless nights of worry. Malcolm Webster would sleep like a baby. The only thing that kept him awake at night was wondering where his next pound was coming from. The magpie-like love of shiny baubles had to be funded somehow, and if it meant drugging, poisoning, killing, fire-raising, so be it.

The strict Victorian hand of his police officer father may have driven him to seek out female rather than male company in later life. He had very few male friends.

The strange goings-on at his family home, with his father

insisting everyone leave the house whenever he needed the loo, must have affected him somehow. He started to set fires at an early age, craving the attention he wasn't getting at home.

Mum Odette, herself a former police officer, was too busy and subjugated to give much of anything to her children. By the time his murderous ways were beginning to unravel, he was even lying to his twin sister Caroline and brother Ian, also a cop.

It's both telling and incredibly sad that he told his own twin sister that he had leukaemia. It speaks of a man devoid of the normal range of emotions. We may lie to friends and acquaintances on a regular basis, but something usually stops us lying to our family members.

The first love who killed herself, according to friends, was the real trigger for Malcolm John Webster to switch off his emotions. He invested in the baubles of everyday life, flung himself into computing at a time when the Internet was a distant dream and computers took up entire rooms, indulged his passion for cars and used those around him to make his life easier.

Second wife Felicity remembers his favourite saying was 'why work hard yourself when someone else could be doing it for you?'

Wherever he went in the world, he was able to mould himself and fit in. In Riyadh, he was invited to the dinner party where he met Felicity; in New Zealand, he found work and lived as part of the extended Drumm family, meeting their friends and family, largely without raising suspicion, with a few notable exceptions.

In Oban, he became treasurer and secretary of the local angling club. Any club choosing a treasurer would think twice about character before rubber stamping an appointment. Webster was given this post readily as nobody considered he was anything other than a man to be trusted.

He repaid that trust in him by robbing them blind.

It is his ordinariness that scares us, the fact that, when we look at him, we are unsure of whether we could have been able to see through the smokescreen.

It's difficult to see how.

Professor David Wilson, a former prison governor, spent years face to face with men like Malcolm Webster. He held the keys to the cells that contained them and draws on that hands-on knowledge as Professor of Criminology and Director of the Centre for Applied Criminology at Birmingham City University. He has written extensively on serious criminality and the mindset behind it. He has worked as a criminal profiler on a number of high-profile UK cases.

At just 29, Wilson became the youngest prison governor in England. He worked at Grendon, Wormwood Scrubs and at Woodhill in Milton Keynes – where he designed and ran two units for the twelve most violent prisoners in the country. This brought him into daily contact with virtually every modern-day serial killer this country has known.

He is immersed in his subject like no other in the country at the present time. A vibrant, well-spoken Scot, Wilson draws on his experiences with some of the country's most violent men to write books on serial killers like Peter Tobin and to lend his considerable expertise to the authorities.

He studied Malcolm Webster and his crime map for this book. His findings are striking.

'Webster most immediately conforms to that type of murderer which we more readily associate with a woman – the black widow, so called because they kill husbands and lovers so as to gain financially and materially from their deaths,' he explained. 'This can be through inheriting their former partner's estate, or simply through the assurance on their partner's life. Webster can therefore be seen as a black widower. Of course, his ability to move from one partner to another also reveals other aspects of his underlying personality.

'Most immediately, it tells us that he has good social skills;

that he can be charming when the occasion demands; and that, as a consequence, people feel attracted to him. He's a seducer, but of course this seduction masks his real intentions.

'These intentions are obviously focused on his own needs – he's selfish and self-centred, and we often associate this type of parasitic lifestyle with those individuals whom we call psychopaths. However, I often feel that this label confuses, because at a "common sense" level people imagine that it would be easy to spot a psychopath, and therefore easy to avoid them.

'Unfortunately, it isn't as easy as that. The reality is that people with this underlying antisocial personality disorder have glib, superficial, easy charms which others will find attractive. If we fail to understand this, we will fail to really understand why Webster was successful.

'I also feel we need to acknowledge another aspect of Webster's personality – his callousness. After all, he had to be prepared to harm his former wives and partners without that affecting his own behaviour.

'He was inured to their pain and suffering, even though he was subsequently able to fake, for example, concern for their well-being and then bereavement.

'We call this "shallow affect". In other words, he knows how he should act, but in reality does not really possess genuine feelings that would prompt these reactions. He has simply learned – as an actor might learn his lines – that this is what is expected of him in these circumstances. Everything for him exists at a surface level – there is no depth to his behaviour.'

As a leading expert taking a scientific approach to the man and his crimes, Wilson is careful about the words he uses to describe offenders. So Webster is a black widower, displaying sociopathic and psychopathic tendencies, but is he a serial killer, or even one in the making, as some who investigated him suggest?

187

Wilson said, 'With this type of murderer I always think – where would it end?

'In other words, how many partners do they need? How much money do they want? Is there a limit that they could ever reach that would make them want to stop? I can't be certain, but I always get the impression that people like Webster are limitless – which is why we should always be grateful when they are caught.'

Shallow affect is described in psychopathy journals as 'emotional poverty or a limited range or depth of feelings, interpersonal coldness in spite of signs of open gregariousness'.

That sentence could have been written to describe Webster. There is also an acknowledged psychopathy checklist used by clinicians around the globe. It was devised by Robert Hare and the list makes for uncomfortable reading when tallied with what we know of Webster: superficial charm, sense of self-worth, pathological lying, cunning and a failure to accept responsibility coupled with a need for stimulation in early life, a parasitic lifestyle and promiscuous sexual behaviour can all be applied to the man and his crimes.

Professor Wilson feels there is a requirement to be cautious, as Webster was caught relatively early in his 'career', even though it took police so long to catch up with him.

Those emotionally involved, who lost loved ones and were conned out of life savings, or whose homes and properties were razed by fires started by Webster, have no such qualms. They all fell victim to him, and they all know what he is: a murdering psychopath who wrecked countless lives across the decades.

What motivates a man – outwardly amiable, articulate and friendly – to pursue, marry, then murder a beautiful young woman?

For the man tasked with bringing Malcolm Webster to justice, the answer was clear: money. DCI Phil Chapman revealed, 'We put together a profile of an individual whose thirst for money was incredible, his ability to spend unprecedented.'

The detective and his team delved back in time, tracing the people who knew Webster best – family, friends, former classmates and his best man. At every point of his life, a similar pattern emerged: Webster was consumed by the desire for money.

Chapman said, 'Within months of Claire's death he had spent everything – about £200,000.

'I'm not a psychologist but any normal person who came into that sort of money would – from my own point of view – pay off their biggest debt, like their mortgage. But he never put a penny into that and in six months he had spent everything.

'He was described by witnesses as charming, witty, gregarious and benevolent – good at remembering birthdays and lavishing people with gifts.

'It appeared his whole drive was purely the status associated with being able to do this.

'A lot of people said it was beyond that and that he was overly generous. Felicity said this too and she said it made her feel uncomfortable.

'Malcolm was outwardly the life and soul of the party but when you scrape away that veneer you have an individual with an outstanding ability to manipulate people, who has told outright lies, convincing people he had a terminal illness.

'We went through this guy's life, all the way back to school. His behaviour was consistent; even his best man said he was a downright liar. He told his own family he had a fatal illness. He told Felicity and others that he had childhood leukaemia and was infertile.

'He shaved his head and eyebrows and showed people puncture marks on his arm. That's not the behaviour of an individual who cares for somebody, telling his nearest and dearest horrible lies.'

Even as police closed the net, Webster hid behind a mask of indifference.

'Malcolm is an extremely astute individual, quite prepared to go along with police, a model prisoner in terms of his behaviour. On only a few occasions did he come close to revealing what, I would suggest, was the true Malcolm, someone willing to pursue a female to the point of engaging in a romantic relationship and ultimately marrying her, solely for the purpose of using her as a vehicle to make money.

'We could see similar patterns of behaviour from his time with the women in his life, an affectionate individual who had underlying behaviour which could rear its head when things weren't going his way.

'Witnesses said he had a look, a sinister look, which could make people feel very uncomfortable. A lot of people don't have wills but Malcolm and the new women in his life had wills within a very short time, of which he was the beneficiary. Many people deal with grief in different ways. His was to start relationships and engage in sexual behaviour within weeks of the death of Claire.'

An incredible insight into the mind of the man from the cop who was tasked with hunting him down and putting him away, it reveals the true nature of the beast, from a copper's cold hard stare.

Webster could deceive all the women he wanted, but, when he was in a room with hardened cops who knew every trick in the book, he was lost. He had to play their game, their way, and so he retreated into himself and became pliant, malleable to the inquiry.

He knew he would maximise his chances of once again escaping the hook by keeping his mouth firmly shut. That Chapman and his team brought together so much evidence against him is testament to the skills of all those involved.

It was so good Webster had nowhere to turn, no wriggle

room. The cold-case cops had, for once in his life, rendered Malcolm Webster speechless.

The science, a series of damning statements and Malcolm Webster's lies had all joined forces against him to prove he was lying about events that night. Events that cost a bright young girl her life, cost an insurance company a small fortune at the time and would eventually, following the Crown prosecution, cost Malcolm Webster, the Black Widower, his freedom.

17

THE SILK'S ROAD

DEREK OGG QC IS ONE OF SCOTLAND'S PRE-EMINENT SILKS, with a passion for the law and learning that is awe-inspiring. He is also the last man you want to see standing opposite you in a court of law.

With Webster, Ogg says he knew from the very beginning, as in every other case, that small steps would eventually lead to them scaling this Everest of evidence.

'It was huge. Biggest case of my life, by some distance. The logistics of it were incredible. The timescale was incredible, as were the time zones. It was a behemoth of a case, and my job was to pull it into bite-sized chunks, jigsaw pieces, that a jury could join together in court.'

Ogg sits on government legal panels and is a specialist in hate crime. But really, he's a specialist in anything he cares to be. 'If I'm running a case where there is specialist knowledge, like a fire for example, I will make sure I know as much as the expert in court on that day about spread of fire, rate of fire, seat of fire, components, etc. I will, for that evidence, know as much as the expert before me, having closeted myself away for weeks in the library doing a crash course. After the case, I can forget about all I have learned. It's a very handy skillset to have, and my memory helps in that process.'

With Webster, Ogg knew he had to produce a play for the audience, a triptych almost, in three parts, covering Claire, Felicity and Simone.

Add to this the damning financial evidence and that of the specialists and it was a more straightforward, although still daunting, prospect. All of these jigsaw pieces lashed together would create the finished answer, a clear picture of a killer.

'Sometimes with juries you have to lead them through the evidence and punctuate your most important points,' Ogg explained. 'It's not cheating or showmanship, it means that you can, for example give them a vital piece of evidence say, just before lunch, so the defence has no chance to jump in.

'We did that with a home videotape Felicity's sister had found in a recorder she had bought from her. Felicity had been financially stripped bare by Webster, but she's a proud woman so, rather than take charity handouts from her family, she was selling things she really didn't need in an effort to make ends meet.

'Her sister bought the video camera and found some footage inside of a party showing Felicity and the family at a garden party of some kind. Malcolm was evidently filming as he was never in shot.

'As she watched this footage, a strange dirge-like music started playing over the footage, footage showing Felicity sitting happily chatting to her friends and family.

'It was the Celtic dirge music from the movie *Titanic*, from the scene where the dead bodies were floating in the water after the boat had sunk. It sent a shiver down her spine and to this day nobody knows how it got on there. It had to be Malcolm.

'I got that evidence to the jury just before lunchtime then asked for the tape to be played. It was strong evidence that Webster was not a normal man. I was told after the trial that, as the jury filed out for lunch after that tape was played, one of them was heard to mutter "the bastard".

'That may seem unfair to some – that we would time things so dramatically – but at times you have to make the point as strongly as possible and leave your opposite number with as little as possible to work with.'

His views on Webster are unequivocal. 'I have never met anyone like him. He is a psychopath. He can mimic emotion but not actually register it. More importantly, he was able to get strong women to fall for him. Remember, these women were not mugs. He worked his way around them slowly but surely.

'The evidence that we heard in court was a man who couldn't stop himself. I have no idea what goes on in that man's mind. I have not, even after 30 years in criminal law, met anyone like him.

'These were all incredibly competent, capable women, they were all caregivers and they'd all reached a certain age in life, I guess, where they might have wondered, "When am I going to get a life?"

'Along comes Malcolm Webster, charming, generous, kind. He says, "Put your feet up. Let *me* do that." He says, "Let *me* make you dinner." He says, "Let *me* give you a massage." "Take this present." And suddenly, the caregiver is being cared for and people said to me how could it be that all these sensible women all fell for this man? For someone to offer to care for you is incredibly, in my judgement, an incredibly seductive thing to do and who doesn't want to be looked after?

'We dug deep into his family life, for an answer, looked at his relationship with his mother, looked at siblings, but there is nothing there that screams at you, apart from a very strange father with some odd ways. Maybe that turned him towards women, strong women, unlike his mother, who had been so dominated and isolated by Alexander Webster that only seven people turned up for her funeral.

'At one point in the trial, I cracked a joke about him being the only straight male nurse in the hospital, something along those lines, so no wonder he was able to hook women.

'It was said in jest but there is a truth to it also, even though the joke fell on deaf ears. The point is he was quite a rarity, in that he was a heterosexual man working in a predominantly female world where even the men who chose that profession tended to be gay. It was relatively easy for him to pick and choose, and it meant he could single women of means out for special attention, which made them feel like they were the pick of the crop, given he had so many to choose from.

'He had no criminal record as a child, no social work involvement, nothing. He had the nickname Pyro and we knew he had developed a love of fire. He used to carry matches everywhere. His other favourite was to carry nail varnish remover around with him as it was his preferred method of starting fires. That's how he set the fire at the home of Felicity's parents.

'Getting him to court was the first hurdle to be overcome. We thought we knew what he had done and how he had done it, but there were issues of getting the evidence and jurisdiction, not to mention what the charges would be.

'He committed murder in Scotland, attempted the same in New Zealand then returned to this country for his third plot. We were faced with a separate jurisdiction in New Zealand; it was something of a master stroke to charge him with an ongoing fraud. Had he not transferred the money he stole from Felicity Drumm to his Scottish bank account, we would not have been able to include the New Zealand evidence at the Scottish trial. It was vital to the case and that's how we did it.

'Some of the people in the team thought we would struggle also to get the charges to stick re his bigamous intent with Simone. Again, as soon as he bought the ring and she had bought a dress, the intent was there and we were able to include that evidence also.

'He is a very clever man. I have no doubt in my mind he

went to the other side of the world to commit his crimes against Felicity specifically because he knew that was where he could get away with it. Nobody joined up the dots back then like they do now. It would not be possible in this day and age to achieve that, but back then it was a simpler world. How much do you know about New Zealand, really?

'He went there with one purpose in mind, to kill Felicity and steal her money. He even bought return tickets for him and his son, and a one-way ticket for her. Unbelievable. There is so much we still do not know about Malcolm Webster. He had gap years in his timeline. He went to New Zealand and Australia as a teenager and again in later life, after the death of Claire.

'He told friends he had worked with Aboriginal children in the Outback. In Abu Dhabi, three children under the age of six died of cardiac arrest and Webster was the nurse on duty who found all three of them. This was over a six-month period. He was suspended and placed under investigation.

'During that investigation, it became apparent, due to his low blood sugar, that he had been injecting himself with insulin to make himself unwell. There was an internal inquiry. His father, the detective chief superintendent in charge of the Fraud Squad, pulled strings to get him out of the country, with the assistance of the Foreign Office.

'He was allowed to leave. We searched and searched, but there are no records of him having ever been in that country. There are photos that exist that show him there, but not according to the authorities there.'

Nobody from the Abu Dhabi Health Authority would return calls or emails in relation to Webster, despite repeated attempts.

Ogg added, 'His time in Oban, equally, should have sounded enough alarm bells for a reopening of the car fire "accident" that killed his first wife.

'To my certain knowledge there was a fire at a home he was living in when he first arrived there, the home of a good friend no less, and there was even a fire at the hospital where he worked. He also stole a laptop computer from that hospital and plundered the accounts of the local fishing club, where he had somehow managed to get himself elected as treasurer.

'With the fire at the Oban & District Hospital, he blamed a patient for smoking. The consultant knew this could not be true, the patient did not have the mental faculty to smoke a cigarette, and he called in police. The charges were later dropped. Perhaps Daddy had intervened again, who knows.

'At the beginning of every day in court, it was only ever me and him. He was always polite and civil to the staff. He was switched off most of the time in the dock, away somewhere else. After his family came to court and gave their evidence that he had contacted them, and tried to kill himself after his deception with Simone emerged, he began to cry in the dock. I was constantly under pressure to have him remanded, but that was never my way. People were angry that he was able to walk in and out of court each and every day. I wanted that. I wanted people to see how calm he was each and every morning. Only someone incapable of feeling emotion could remain that calm as events like these whirled around him.

'When I was a younger solicitor, I made a promise to myself that I would never have someone remanded ahead of a guilty verdict unless it was absolutely essential and unavoidable. Can you imagine if that was the night before you are due to give the most important evidence on the most important day of your life and you're afraid, surrounded by nutters, screaming the place down around you? You would turn up at court unshaven, unkempt, tired. It would not have been fair. But after he broke down in the dock I began to reconsider that position and in the last week of the trial I asked that he be remanded.

'I felt he could have ended his own life as the ultimate control gesture, or that he would do his usual and disappear. Control was what drove Webster. Think of all the women in his life, all the women we found. Every single one of them, without fail, were taken on long drives along rural country roads.

'He got a kick out of holding that steering wheel in his hand and thinking, "With one flick of my wrists on this steering wheel, I can end your life." If I had killed the woman I loved in a car crash, you would never see me behind the wheel again. It was a matter of days later that Webster bought himself a 4X4 and was showing it off to friends.

'Antiques, watches, paintings, you name it. There is money somewhere, in storage, that only he knows about. I'm sure he has it stored away hoping that at some point he can get out and revel in it all again. We couldn't find any money, but knowing his love of all things antique, the magpie that is Webster will have squirreled some of it away.

'It would have been nice to find it for Felicity. Alas, not yet.

'There is also a strong suspicion among officers that Webster may have had some sexual motive in drugging the women he was with. The ultimate control. We shall never truly know, unless he tells us.'

Ogg revealed a little-known case in Scots law had given him the confidence to proceed with the case against Webster. In typical Ogg fashion, it dates from 1972.

Helga Konrad, 18, had arrived in Edinburgh from Germany with Ernest Dumoulin, the 21 year old she had met through a lonely hearts advert. They had run away together, and decided Scotland was where they would spend their lives.

At least Helga believed that. Ernest had other ideas.

On Friday, 13 October 1972, the couple married in a register office service witnessed by Herbert Wood and his wife, the couple in charge of the Torphichen Street guesthouse where the young couple were staying.

It was a pleasant ceremony followed by coffee, a few celebratory drinks and then a meal at a restaurant in Shandwick Place.

It was the early hours of the next morning when a knock on the guesthouse front door roused Mr Wood from his bed.

Two grim-faced detectives and a dazed-looking Dumoulin, his right arm bandaged and his suit smeared with mud, were standing there.

A seaman had been strolling along the foot of Salisbury Crags before something caught his eye. It was the corpse of a woman.

He ran to find police and soon after they found Dumoulin.

He said they had gone for a romantic walk up the Crags, but Helga had lost her footing and she plunged down the rocky crags to her death.

Dumoulin retired to his room in the guesthouse, playing the same record over and over, the haunting theme of the Hollywood film *Love Story*.

When police took him away for more questioning, proprietor Mrs Woods seized the chance to 'clean' the young German's room. There, she came across a letter to Dumoulin from an insurance company and a receipt. It revealed details of a £412,000 insurance policy taken on Helga's life just days before she died.

Dumoulin had obtained a car under false pretences while in Germany and sold it for £650. He had lodged £250 of it in the Bank of Nova Scotia in Princes Street, obtaining £10,000 of credit in the process. He then used that credit to take out a string of insurance policies to cover his young wife's life.

Incredibly, Dumoulin barely waited until his wife's body was cold before he approached the insurance company the morning after her fall to stake his claim. He was told they would not pay out because Helga had been 'killed on a mountain'.

Police now had their motive.

Of course, Dumoulin denied it all. He was charged with murder and appeared at the High Court in Edinburgh, where he claimed his teenage bride had tried to kill him and that, by the grace of God, he had been saved, while she had fallen.

However, when Hambro Life Assurance confirmed that the life insurance policy Dumoulin had taken out in Helga's name would have cost a massive £442 a month to maintain, the jury's minds were made up.

Ernest Dumoulin was found guilty of murdering his wife of only a few hours and was sentenced to life imprisonment.

A memorial seat sits in the shadow of Salisbury Crags, a metal plate on it commemorating her short life: 'In loving memory of our daughter, Helga Konrad, born 16.6.54, died 13.10.72. Buried at Schwerbach, Germany, only 300 yards from her parents' home.'

It was a tragic love story gone wrong for those directly affected by it. For Derek Ogg, the comparisons to Webster made it a precedent. Dumoulin had begun his criminal endeavour in Germany but concluded it in Scotland. He had moved money from Germany to Scotland and banked it. The Dumoulin case of 1972 was what persuaded Derek Ogg that Webster could be tried in Scotland, despite the geography of his criminal career.

'It was a tragic case but very similar to ours in so many ways. He argued he should have been tried in Germany, where the crime began and was born, if you like, but the financial side of the offence, and the body, gave Scotland jurisdiction.'

Ogg added, 'I'll never see another case like Webster. At least I hope I don't. I called him a cruel, practised deceiver, a clever man who would go on to kill again and was a danger to women. The judge and the jury agreed. Even his defence QC, I think, agreed. There's only one man on earth who disagrees: Malcolm Webster.

'If ever the saying a wolf in sheep's clothing applied to anybody, it was Webster.

'It became obvious to me that he was a very clever criminal. Although he didn't have formal educational qualifications, he was someone who had a bent for acting.

'He was a man who had an innate cleverness. Remember

always in your minds that this is a man who made his wife's murder look like an accident.'

Mr Ogg said Webster had few male friends, with the number of female witnesses a stand-out feature of the trial.

'The victims were all women of a certain age and all women who had given their careers to the care of other people.

'He would make them laugh and do little things of kindness and consideration. Here was someone who said, "Let me care for you." That was the Rock Hudson moment. It wasn't his fantastic looks or his money. It was his ability to say to hard-working, experienced caregivers, "Here is someone to care for you."

'They were vulnerable to nothing at all, perhaps except only to that.'

The QC got his man, and gladly accepted the pats on the back for a job well done. And so he should. Ogg and his team took a horrific case and boiled it down to its essence. That essence was that here was a man who killed and lied and burned for money. All for money. Ogg let the experts talk the jury through it all.

Perhaps more importantly, he let the women targeted by Webster tell it in their own words. It worked better than even he could have imagined.

Webster must have known from a very early stage in the trial that all hope was lost. Even his QC, Edgar Prais, a skilled orator and silk, could muster nothing substantial in defence of his client. Prais was not even in court when the jury returned their verdict. It was his last case. He retired on that very day.

He can take comfort from the fact that he never really had a chance.

18

RELIEF

FELICITY DRUMM, SIMONE BANARJEE AND THE FAMILY OF Claire Morris all cried when the jury returned the guilty verdicts, a vindication of all they had come to court to say.

For Felicity, a 30-year sentence for the man who systematically targeted, robbed and tried to murder her was the closure she needed.

She is a nurse, a carer, and the mother of Malcolm Webster's son. Not physically big, she carries a big heart and soul in her small frame. At times during the global murder inquiry, she cried herself out, her pale-blue eyes had no more tears to give, and had shrunk back in her skull somewhat, as if scared to look any more at the horrors being uncovered all around her.

She has spent her life caring for other people as an oncology nurse, both in Auckland, New Zealand, and in Saudi Arabia, where she first encountered the man she would go on to marry.

What she lacks in height she makes up for in strength of conviction. Her eyes have steeled somewhat since her encounter with the black widower, and she herself admits the days of falling in love 'Mills & Boon style' are long gone. He stole that from her.

But she has survived where others did not, and she is thankful for that.

Takapuna, where she lives with her extended family, is a small but affluent suburb in Auckland, and everyone is a neighbour. Her straightforward Kiwi character has helped to shape her and get her through the last 12 years. Lesser women would have collapsed, but Felicity Drumm had a son to think of, Edward, who now prefers to be called Ned. He is the only remaining bond between her and Webster, a 13-year-old boy mad on rugby and computer PlayStation games who knows his dad is in jail, and why. He has been taunted at school by the other kids yelling, 'Your dad's a murderer.'

He lay asleep in the bedroom next door as Felicity took the call telling her that his father, the murderer, would never be free again. She didn't wake him.

During her evidence at the High Court, it became clear very quickly that this was a woman with nothing to tell but the truth. She told it concisely, in a way that only victims of such horrors can. They have lived with it for so long they find emotional shorthand to describe it to others hearing it for the first time.

The jurors who listened to her story were gobsmacked, just as police in New Zealand had been when they sat her down with a cuppa and listened to her telling of the saga.

It was a huge outpouring of emotion, a story that, when it was proved to be a true account, started a manhunt that would see Webster dragged before his peers in a Scottish court of law and thrown in jail for life.

She is still working as an oncology nurse in New Zealand, helping and caring for people struck down by cancer. Some might wonder how anyone could function after everything she has endured. Surely, the ability to care for others must somehow have been tarnished after the events laid out in court.

Fortunately, she doesn't feel like that. Her testimony was clear, concise and utterly damning as any evidence ever heard in court. She was the prosecution's star witness, because she was alive to tell the tale, and she had sparked the entire investigation.

She pursued Webster for one simple reason: to stop it happening to anyone else. She had lost her life savings and almost her life to him, yet she was once again motivated by her caring gene. She even refused to divorce him as the inquiry developed because she feared that would leave him open to target and remarry other women.

She didn't know it at that time, but he had already become engaged to Simone in Oban, on the west coast of Scotland, and was desperate to be rid of Felicity, who refused to countenance any suggestion of divorce. After so many years of controlling and dominating her, Webster was in a place he hated: she had the control over him.

And, at the end of it all, after the phone call, there were a few tears and deep breaths, and messages of support from family. She had done it. It had taken 12 years of her life, but she had got him.

'It was a huge moment for me because I finally felt free from Malcolm Webster,' Felicity recalled. 'I was a bit tearful because after getting the verdict from a jury who had heard all the evidence it just struck me, the enormity of what I had been through.

'It's fantastic that justice has been done for Claire, myself and Simone – Malcolm has been publicly recognised for the terrible things he has done.

'It's been a very long 12 years for me and after I gave my evidence I was on a real high because I felt liberated from Malcolm.

'There have been many sleepless nights. I hope now that Claire and her family can find peace.

'It's all about control with Malcolm. When he doesn't have that complete control, he goes into meltdown. I'm convinced that's why he drugged me repeatedly. It was all about the power.

'I am sickened and repulsed by him now. I just can't believe that somebody you cared about could be capable of doing all the things he did.

'I feel very lucky to be alive.'

Felicity's sister Jane Drumm said the family was 'really delighted' with the verdict, and the 30-year sentence. 'It closes a book. This has been 12 years.'

Six family members had given evidence against Webster. 'We all felt that we did our best and it is great. We feel validated now. Justice has been given to my sister and to Claire and her family, and to my parents.

'He can't hurt any other women. It was really devastating. There were a number of times where we could easily have lost my sister. There were a number of attempts on her life and to me it was just amazing good fortune we have still got her and it is amazing good fortune we have still got my parents.

'It took a lot out of my parents and my sister. She was left completely cleaned out financially with a little child. She has got on and remade her life. Trying to remember back 12 years ago was hard for all of us and there was a lot of pressure to do the right thing and perform well during the trial. It is such a big relief.'

Felicity said, 'When I heard that he'd been arrested in Guildford in 2008 it was a massive relief.

'I will always be extremely grateful to Jane for all her help because, before she mentioned it to the officer, in Leeds in 2006, we had pretty much given up hope that Malcolm would ever be brought to justice.'

Jane added, 'We are all just thrilled that it's all finally over for us because we have waited years.

'When the police in Scotland refused to reopen the case into Claire's death, we pretty much gave up hope of ever getting justice and tried to rebuild our lives.

'It has taken a terrible toll on my parents; they are both in their eighties now. I am just delighted that they were able to see Malcolm being sent to prison.

'I think it is more good fortune than anything else that nobody else was killed before Malcolm was finally caught, so I'm pleased that he is in a position now that he can't do any more harm to so many people.

'Malcolm must have been like this from a very early age and it makes me really angry that his family did nothing to stop it or help Felicity and her son – they must have had suspicions for a very long time that something was wrong with Malcolm.'

Since the trial, Felicity and son Ned have managed to put Webster behind them and have 'prospered' in the wake of the guilty verdicts.

Felicity's sister Jane said his crimes seemed to be motivated by a need to appear rich and powerful. He courted multiple women at the same time before Felicity agreed to marry him. 'He was like a paedophile, grooming women and seeing which one he could get across the line. Any one of those women could have ended up dead.'

Felicity is a lot calmer than one would expect, given recent events in her life. She has an inner strength that shines out through her pale-blue eyes and connects with the world around her. You can tell she is a carer; her face is marked with the lines of worry, laughter and grief. She is open, honest and decent; she was just unlucky enough to give herself to the wrong man.

'I think that things, possessions and people, are expendable if they meet his ultimate need,' she said. 'I have spent, at different times, a lot of time agonising over what was real and what wasn't. "Did I ever mean anything to him? Was I purely a meal ticket right from the start?"

'Because Claire lost her life, I've had the opportunity to rebuild mine. But, very sadly for her and her family, that's an opportunity lost, and all along it's been about getting justice for her, as well as myself.

'Malcolm had a very good sense of humour. He could be

very personable, very attentive. I think that one of his skills, and one of the reasons for such success, is that he makes a study of the people he's around, establishes what their interests are and then adopts them so that you find all these things that you have in common.

'I wouldn't say he was the only true love of my life, but I loved him. I think there was a huge element of control. I think he drugged me because he could, and he somehow got off on that and it was a game to him.

'My only regret is that his parents were not alive to see him brought to justice. I mean that.'

Claire Morris's brother Peter, who has become firm friends with Felicity, added: 'If Webster hadn't done what he did in New Zealand, we wouldn't be where we are now. Felicity was the most precious witness in the whole trial. I have an enormous amount of respect for her. She told me her primary objective was to get justice for Claire.'

Felicity is in talks with a New Zealand TV company to make a dramatisation of her life with Malcolm Webster. The Black Widower left her penniless, despite a lifetime of working and saving hard to give herself some financial independence.

With a child to support, and no prospect of any help from Webster, she faces the unpleasant reality that, while she would like to forget and move on, she has to take the opportunities available to her in an effort to safeguard the future.

She is starting again. She knows she is lucky to be in that position. If Webster had had his way, she would not be around to tell her story.

'He took everything. I can't even afford to divorce him. The procurator fiscal checked Malcolm's finances to see if there is anything that could be awarded to me, but there's nothing left. He hasn't a penny to his name. I've been told that Malcolm is now bankrupt in all but name, it just needs to be made official.'

The end of the case also gave Felicity a chance to meet the only other survivor in Webster's trail of death and destruction,

Simone Banarjee. The women met for the first time in a Glasgow restaurant, in the heart of the west end. Simone was alone and Felicity was being clucked around by family. Then they watched a movie together.

Counselling sessions have helped Simone put Webster and her relationship with him behind her, and she remains a lovely, caring woman, determined to get on with her life.

She has a tight circle of friends, and she still sails. Recently, her boat slipped its mooring and drifted up the west coast for a short while with nobody on board. Amazingly, it found its way to another mooring none the worse for its pilotless adventure. That's about as much excitement as Simone wants in her life after what she has been through, but it may just show the tide is turning, and a little bit of luck is finally coming her way.

When Peter and Betty Morris heard the guilty pleas it was the beginning of the end, the closure required to bring this tragic chapter of their lives to an end. Nobody else would suffer from the 'psychological sadism' Webster peddled ever again, Peter announced.

He added, on the steps of the court, 'I hope this will apply to anyone else involved with Malcolm Webster, that they also feel relieved and elated by the conclusion arrived at today. They are now free.'

Peter feels Webster could have gone on to become one of the country's most notorious serial killers, just like Dr Harold Shipman, whom Webster studied. 'I believe he is still dangerous. Even when the case was reopened, he was still grooming a woman called Ann.'

As we have seen, Ann Hancock also received a letter warning her that her life was in danger because of her relationship with the killer.

Peter added, 'While he was living with Ann, he had plans to go on some medical course which was to do with suicide and assisted death. One can only imagine the consequences – how he could have perverted going on that course to killing people, and then saying they'd wanted it to happen. The potential for a serial killer is enormous.'

Peter spoke of the heartbreak Webster had caused his family. 'Not only did he kill Claire, he caused the mutilation and destruction of her body so we weren't even able to say a proper goodbye or pay our last respects to her. He even took future girlfriends to Claire's grave, recounting the details of the crash to gain their sympathy.

'I'm elated he was found guilty. I didn't expect to feel that.'

He continued, 'Justice for Claire is a big thing for Mum. She has asked me to say that Claire was a very happy and full-of-life person. And that she greatly misses Claire, who was her best friend.'

Peter announced the family was to create a new headstone for their beloved Claire, one that did not feature the words: 'Beloved wife of Malcolm'.

There was only one problem. The plot was owned by Webster, and Peter was told he would need the killer's permission to change it.

Webster, sitting inside HMP Barlinnie, alone and afraid, clung on to the last vestige of control he had and refused to give that permission. The family were incensed. Not only did he refuse permission, he signalled clearly that the plot was where he would also be buried when he died.

The murderer would be laid to rest beside his victim. It was almost too much for Betty Morris to bear. Her son Peter had to protect her from this type of devastating revelation, while at the same time either force Webster into a U-turn or find another way, some legal route, to get his wish.

If he failed, his sister would spend eternity under a plaque drawn by her killer. And when he died, he would join her.

The row over the plaque was perhaps Webster's best opportunity to apologise, grant permission and do his time. It was a perfect moment for him to send a message to the family that he accepted his heinous crimes and was prepared to help ease their suffering.

Not a chance. He has refused to this day to give up the plot. He sees no reason why he should. He is an innocent man, in his own eyes.

Peter enlisted the help of a team of young student lawyers from the University of Aberdeen, who helped him battle Aberdeenshire Council in a bid to have something done about the situation. The news made headlines around the world, so strange and perverse was it to many decent-minded people.

The inscription on Claire's gravestone in Tarves Cemetery, Aberdeenshire, reads: 'With loving thoughts of my dear wife Claire J Webster.'

Peter said, 'For 17 years, Claire hasn't rested in peace. Until her headstone is changed, I don't think she can. To be told I need to get a murderer's permission is ludicrous. Why should he have any rights?'

Aberdeenshire Council, finding itself in a legal pickle not of its own making, eventually applied a modicum of common sense and compassion, and removed the headstone, placing it in storage, ostensibly until the legal row was resolved. In practical terms, though, it is unlikely it will ever mark Claire Morris's final resting-place again.

Karen Wiles, head of legal and governance at the authority, said, 'We appreciate the strong feelings of Ms Morris's family and the wider public mood about this issue.

'Having considered very carefully all the legal implications, we believe that, given Mr Webster's criminal conviction, it is appropriate for us to remove the headstone and place it in secure storage. We have written to Mr Webster's lawyer asking him to relinquish his position as lair holder and have received a response declining this request.

'We will be writing once again to advise them of the action we have now taken.'

Webster, a beaten man, both literally and figuratively, is using the issue of the headstone to exact revenge on a family for putting him somewhere he does not believe he should be – prison. He will never give it up. He applied for legal aid in 2012 to contest the council's decision and to have the headstone put back. This was refused in mid-March 2012. Webster has the right to appeal the decision, and will no doubt do so.

Peter added, 'The words on that headstone represent a lie. I genuinely believe in my heart that Claire will not rest in peace until that lie is rectified. That headstone is full of lies right across it starting with "Loving thoughts of my dear wife". Malcolm Webster premeditated my sister's murder from the time he started courting her. So the idea that she was a dear wife to him is a fallacy beyond imagination.

'What I'd like to happen is that the headstone carries her maiden name, Claire J. Morris. And the last line about "my constant soul" was a line Malcolm put there. He planned to murder his wife. To then claim she was constantly in his soul is ludicrous.

'It's devious. It's the epitome of all the lies he told and it's represented on that headstone. What I want is the truth to be put on that headstone. That person is Claire Morris, not Claire Webster. I want the reflections of her family and friends to be there so that, in a hundred years' time when we are gone, the truth will still be here, not a lie. That's very important to me. I feel then that my darling sister would be able to rest in peace.'

In spite of the shameful words on her headstone, penned by her killer, her husband, as we have seen, Claire Morris did speak from beyond the grave. A tiny little piece of her remained and that was enough to prove her husband a cold-blooded killer. She loved and laughed in life, but in death she exacted the perfect revenge.

Peter also branded Webster a 'monster'. 'Hopefully, now Claire can rest in peace. I feel that she hasn't been able to do that until now. If the police hadn't caught him the killing would have gone on.'

He said he believed the 30-year term was 'the correct sentence for an extremely dangerous criminal. It's more important that he's taken from society because of the damage he can cause to women.

'I would hate for that to happen to anyone else.'

Peter added, 'I now feel that Claire, who has waited 17 years for this, after her death, will now be able to rest in peace. There is now justice for Claire. The guilty verdict of murder has proven that Malcolm Webster is a wicked murderer. The psychological sadism over me and my family, and many other people, is now broken.

'As the truth came out, it broke the web of deception Malcolm Webster had created around him. Since the reopening of the case in 2008, it has taken approximately three years and three months to arrive at this conclusion.

'During this time, my family and I have experienced every range of emotion which is impossible to convey, but at times it has been a rollercoaster ride. I'm very happy the process is at an end.

'Claire is greatly missed. She was good company. We were proud of Claire becoming a nurse. Her death is devastating. We get upset when we think about how she suffered when she died and are sad at the loss. My mother has lost a daughter and her best friend. I have lost a sister, my dearest sister.'

Peter is trying to ensure that some good comes from the death of his beloved sister, and he wants to establish a foundation in her honour, as a way of protecting the victims of crime. He hopes a £1 million support centre will help to ease the burden of those affected by crime.

Last September, he set off on a walk from her graveside in Aberdeenshire, to the Scottish Parliament in Edinburgh, collecting signatures on a petition as he went. His petition calls on the Scottish Parliament to urge the Scottish Government to consider the need for new legislation and provision to protect, support and assist victims of crime.

He ended up spending a few days in hospital with foot problems halfway along the 150-mile trek. Peter managed to walk the final mile to Parliament, with the help of crutches, having collected over 6,000 signatures, and he handed the petition to Justice Minister Kenny MacAskill.

MSPs then invited him to address a committee on why there should be such a foundation. He left them in no uncertain terms.

Peter told them that Webster had played mind games with them throughout the trial, at one point standing next to him in a courtroom canteen queue. He also sat outside the family waiting room during his trial. Peter says he also smiled and taunted them during a visit to the murder scene. 'I genuinely believe, in his own way, he was trying to provoke me,' he said.

'On three or four occasions, he stood one place behind me in the dining queue. He often sat outside our private waiting room. My son was angry and wanted to say something. My wife was very emotional when he was there at a visit to the scene. I told them to put up an emotional brick wall. I said anything they might do could jeopardise the trial.'

Peter pleaded with MSPs to provide better services for crime victims. He believes bereaved relatives are pulled from 'pillar to post' trying to get information about cases from police. He said that, during the investigation into his sister's killing, he sometimes did not see the liaison officers for months. He told MSPs he wants police forces in Scotland to replace family liaison officers with 'case companions' who would work more closely with grieving relatives, as 'this would indicate to the family that they have someone who is on their side, who is a friend and not just working for police purposes.

'I would suggest at least a once-a-week phone call while the investigation is going on just to check on the wellbeing of the victims' families.'

On four occasions, prior to an arranged police visit to his 86-year-old mother, Peter had to take her to an A&E department because she had extremely high blood pressure. After that, he agreed with police he would 'gently' pass information about the case on to his mother, rather than have officers contact her. 'There were many times throughout the process, the very long process, that I genuinely didn't think she was going to survive,' he recalled.

'A much more victim-friendly approach needs to be taken by the police.

'I fully respect the accused is innocent until proved guilty but I genuinely think they should be kept in a separate part of a courthouse because the ability of jeopardising a trial because of somebody's inappropriate actions is quite high.'

He also criticised the Victims' Commissioner for England and Wales, Louise Casey, for saying a survey of 400 murder trials had shown that most families wanted to be left alone after the events, and added, 'For me, that showed a complete lack of empathy about the subject she was addressing. Of course they want to be left alone, they're in pain but you wouldn't leave a cancer victim alone because they're in pain. You would give them every possible opportunity and treatment to try to help them recover.

'When you're waiting for the truth about your loved one, one of the things which is very frustrating and causes mistrust is when an eternity of time is spent getting an answer to a question.

'The public have backed my campaign and it seems to be resonating with the politicians as well.'

Perhaps the most galling, especially in his efforts to protect his 86-year-old mum from some of the harsher aspects of the case, was the letter she received from the Criminal Injuries Compensation Board.

Not only did it tell her the claim for her daughter's death, a paltry £11,000 in compensation – which Betty considered an insult anyway – was time-barred, but also, unbelievably, they addressed the letter to 'Betty Webster'.

Peter said, 'They addressed the letter to "Dear Mrs Webster" – in the killer's name. They described her as "Betty Webster, applicant". It was the most insensitive thing they could do.'

It wasn't until February 2011 that Peter was told he had just two weeks left to make a compensation claim. 'We were told that, from the time someone is charged, there's a two-year period for making an application. That was February this year. Webster was charged in February 2009.

'When I discussed it with my mother, she initially said £11,000 was an insult for Claire's life and wouldn't bring her back. She refused. After about a month, she agreed I could make an application on her behalf because I persuaded her it was money she was entitled to.'

However, despite letters of support from Victim Support Scotland and the Crown Office, it was refused.

Peter said, 'I'm going to be appealing vehemently. I'm going to be complaining about the way my mother was treated.

'They have shown no regard for a bereaved family member. Why do people have to go through this kind of ordeal? This is another example of how victims are treated as second-class citizens.'

The slap in the face, hard on the heels of the furore caused by the headstone outrage and Webster's refusal to give up his rights to it, has shaken Betty Morris to her core.

Sadly, there was more bad news to come. The damage caused to his foot during his mammoth walk to the Scottish Parliament in her memory resulted in his having to have part of his leg amputated. Gangrene set in to the affected right leg and he had to have it removed to save his life.

Bravely, Peter said, 'I'd do it again. If I can make changes, or help to make some changes through the Victims' Rights Bill which is going through Holyrood at the moment then this will have been worthwhile. It means that for ever and a day people will benefit from this, and that's more important than my right leg. I woke up this morning and I'm so happy to be alive. If they hadn't amputated my leg, it would have killed me.'

The strength and bravery of Webster's victims and their families puts him to shame.

19

FIRE TO CLEANSE

WITH THE CHILDHOOD NICKNAME PYRO, IT WAS PERHAPS inevitable that Malcolm Webster would fall back on familiar territory when it came to masking his crimes.

Fire holds a strange fascination for man, even more so the young at heart. Who doesn't enjoy a good fire, be it indoors or outside on an otherwise chilly evening. We have learned to control fire, an ancient life force, and have evolved to use it to our advantage.

Malcolm Webster certainly did that. The extent of his fire-raising can only mean he is an arsonist as well as a killer. Much of the evidence of his fire-raising was never put before the jury at his trial.

Detectives and prosecutors alike feared it would somehow muddy the waters, although it did go to helping them establish a pattern of behaviour. Hard evidence that he was to blame for setting the various fires was hard to pin down so long after the events and Webster, as usual, was giving nothing away.

In fact, they even agreed in court that Webster was not guilty of setting fire to a storage facility in Aberdeen. A fire that earned him over £60,000 in compensation from insurers. A fire that all those involved in the case believe he did indeed start, before returning home to watch live coverage of the blaze as it unfolded on TV. He was only found guilty of fraudulently claiming after the fire.

The murder of his first wife and attempted murder of his second were more important to prosecutors and they allowed the fire charge to slip away, in order that the trial could be hurried along. It still became the longest trial of a single accused person in Scots legal history, and fire was at its very heart.

The prosecuting team believed Webster's use of fire to cover his tracks was incidental in terms of relevance compared to the more heinous crimes he stood accused of, but over the years it had earned him hundreds of thousands of pounds and bought him something far more precious: time.

From igniting nail varnish remover and starting fires as a boy right through to the last known blaze he set, at a hospital in Oban, flame held such a fascination for him, as it had been such an excellent accomplice for so many decades. We will simply never know the true extent of his arson.

In fact, Webster's fascination with flame had been so obsessive that, years later, a man who had attended Scout groups with him when they were schoolboys would feel compelled to write to Scottish Police warning them about his old pal's fire-setting ways.

We do know that the young Webster used flames to impress his peers and to gain attention. He used his mother Odette's nail varnish remover, spread it along various items, and ignited it. He would later use the same technique on the arm of a chair in the living room of Felicity Drumm's parents' home in Takapuna, New Zealand. If they died in the fire, so be it; if they lived, it still bought him time, obfuscated enquiries and silenced probing questions.

It was his killing of first wife Claire where he truly cemented his partnership with fire, using it so effectively that his first wife had to be identified from dental records. He had stocked the jeep with petrol cans and newspapers as she lay sedated in the passenger seat.

That was the beginning of the deadly side of the partnership, as far as we know. Despite cashing in over £200,000 in insurance money at a time when a three-bedroom house cost around £70,000, it was not the end. Just like the infernos he created, Webster always wanted more.

When the world-exclusive story on Malcolm Webster broke, the senior police source who had alerted me to the top-secret inquiry told me, 'Fire follows this guy around. Almost everywhere he has been, there has been a fire. He likes to use it to cover his tracks. He was behind a massive fire in Aberdeen, at a storage facility. It raged for days and was all over the news. It was the biggest fire the brigade had ever dealt with, back at that time. Evidence is thin on the ground as it was so long ago, but we feel he did it.'

When Webster and his second wife Felicity Drumm left the Middle East in the late '90s, they spent a short time in Scotland, before moving to New Zealand. Felicity had just given birth to their son Edward. Everything they owned was being stored at the Shore Porters Society storage facility on the outskirts of Aberdeen. There was a huge blaze at the facility, a short while after Webster had visited to collect a case.

An investigation found that the most probable cause of the blaze was a blowtorch left on the roof by workmen.

What they did not know at that time, and can be revealed here, was that Webster's storage space at Shore Porters was directly underneath the seat of fire.

They were mistaken in their belief that the fire started on the roof. In fact, it started in an area directly below that, the very area for which Webster had a key. He claimed over £87,000 when the true value of his property was closer to £50,000. Insurers finally paid out £68,000 after Webster had complained in the local newspaper that they were dragging their heels over paying out. At his trial, he was convicted of defrauding them of £18,000. A charge that he set the fire was dropped by the Crown.

Grampian Police have always said any fresh evidence would be reinvestigated.

We already know that police and forensic experts were so concerned at Webster's firebug ways that the samples of tissue taken from the corpse of his first wife were moved from the storage facility and placed in the office safe of Dr James Grieve, the man who provided the evidence that was key in convicting Webster.

Chillingly, at that time he had befriended, and bedded, Dr Grieve's computer manager and asked her where such samples would be stored.

However, it was in New Zealand that his fire-raising skills really came into their own; as the pressure of staying one step ahead became too much to bear, fire bought him the time required to flee the country ahead of cops arresting him over his trail of destruction.

As we have seen, upon arriving in New Zealand in 1998, Felicity and Webster stayed with her parents while they searched for a new home of their own. Very quickly, they found the house of their dreams, priced at NZ$600,000. Back then that equated to around £182,000 in sterling.

Webster was to put up half the money. Felicity, who as a single woman had been living mortgage-free with savings in the bank, put up her half almost immediately. Then the excuses, and the fires, started.

Webster had already torched their cottage in Lyne of Skene and the Shore Porters Society facility, and he now turned his attention to the very home Felicity had put a deposit on to buy.

Knowing that he had no intention of buying a house with Felicity, Webster had driven to the home of her dreams in Bayswater, Auckland, in January 1999, soaked newspapers with petrol and shoved them through the letterbox, before dropping a light into them and walking off.

The house they were about to buy was gutted. So was Felicity: 'I was totally bewildered. I couldn't believe that yet again something like this would happen to us. It seemed extraordinary that we'd had such a series of events.'

Felicity was only able to give evidence about these fires because her husband had failed to start the one fire, in the boot of the crashed Honda as they drove to the bank, that would have brought to an end any prospect of a successful criminal prosecution against the Black Widower.

Luckily for her, he did not have time to ignite that one and local police were quickly on the scene.

Buying the house was a stressful time for Felicity. Webster always had an excuse to explain why his share of the money to buy their new home had not come through. On one occasion, he even told her the Scottish banking system was antiquated and that the wheels move slowly in Scotland.

Webster's personal account was with the Clydesdale Bank in Aberdeen, a well-respected Scottish institution slap bang in the middle of one of the biggest oil-driven micro-economies in Europe. Aberdeen is the financial and business hub for some of the world's biggest oil cartels. It is not a 'wee town' by any stretch of the imagination, yet Webster was able to cling to this lie for weeks.

By this time, he had stolen Felicity's savings after persuading her to give him access to her funds with a joint account. He had also taken out and forged her signature on a number of insurance policies. Most galling for her, though, was that he had planned it all as far back as the first fire.

At one point, he told Felicity and her father Brian that the bank had sent a senior employee to New Zealand some days before so that Webster could expedite the process of releasing funds. Nobody saw this banker. It never happened.

Then, in February 1999, as they lay sleeping at her parents' home, a fire started in an upstairs living room in the dead of night, shortly after Webster had got up 'to use the bathroom'.

The ensuing fire could have killed them all.

Felicity said, 'I think he thought it a perfect out. He could walk out of the house with our son and we would all perish inside.'

There were some startling discoveries when forensic accountants picked apart his life and his spending patterns.

For one thing, they discovered Webster bought a petrol can after repeatedly claiming he would never again carry fuel in a car following the fireball car crash death of his first wife.

Felicity found a receipt from an Auckland petrol station in his briefcase. The receipt – dated just two weeks after they had arrived in New Zealand, 3 December 1998 – was for a 10-litre petrol can, bought along with a Crunchie, a *Marie Claire* magazine, a music tape and unleaded petrol. That receipt, more than any other piece of evidence, gave investigators the shivers.

Derek Ogg QC said, 'The calm terror of it, really, is what makes it stand out. Mundane items like a music tape and a Crunchie bar, yet at the same time he knew exactly why he was buying a 10-litre petrol can.'

Webster was challenged in court by Ogg about this. Ogg told the killer he knew 'every item' he had ever bought, all the 'trinkets' and credit-card purchases dating back years.

He also had a killer punchline: 'There is one thing you have never, ever bought . . . a fire extinguisher.'

Felicity and her father had found the receipt while searching through Webster's briefcase on 18 February 1999. Her father had just discovered all her life savings were gone, and believed Webster was about to kill her.

By this time, Felicity had realised the awful truth. She had opened a fixed-rate savings account at her bank and deposited NZ$140,000 on 1 December 1998. By February 1999, there was just NZ$21,640.27 left. Her loving husband, the man who made her smile, had helped himself to the rest. It was sitting in his Clydesdale Bank account in Aberdeen. And it wasn't coming back.

Neither was Webster. As Felicity raced to the police, he raced to the airport. He again ventured to Australia at this point and to the Middle East, but investigators lost track of him, as New Zealand cops issued international arrest warrants.

He surfaced again in Oban, a picture-postcard fishing port on the west coast of Scotland. It didn't take too long to find his next victim, or start his next fire.

However, there was something about this fire that troubled a consultant working at the Lorn & Islands District General Hospital. During the day, a small fire had been started in a waste bin. Webster, by now working as a manual handling nurse, was on duty. In his report, he blamed an elderly patient who he says must have thrown a cigarette into the basket when a member of staff approached.

The consultant who read this report did not believe that for a second. He went straight to police and told them the elderly patient in question was so debilitated by the Alzheimer's that was riddling his mind and body that he would probably not even know what a cigarette was, never mind have the basic motor skills required to put one in his mouth and light it.

At the same time, a laptop went missing from the hospital. Again, Webster was suspected. He was charged with this offence but these charges were later dropped by the Crown. Another chance to bring his life of crime to an end had slipped away.

The home of a friend also went up in smoke while Webster was in Oban. There had been a falling out over money some days previously. Again, there was not enough evidence.

Worst of all, he had used fire to murder his wife Claire in 1994. He set the fire after the first witness raced to a local farm to raise the alarm. Then he watched her die, telling rescuers she was not inside the car, but 'at home in bed'.

The cottage fires, the Shore Porters Society fire, the new Zealand blazes. The car fire and staged fires that he was unable to execute. Fire was a friend to Webster. It gave him the ultimate control. It cleansed his crime scenes and brought him money.

It bought him valuable time when those around him became suspicious of him.

On every occasion when Malcolm Webster needed time to think, or needed money, there was a fire. The true extent of his fire-raising will never be known unless he comes clean and tells all, now that he is safely behind bars. Investigators are not expecting that to happen any time soon.

They are, however, keeping a very close eye on him, as prison guards know that those obsessed with fire rarely stop.

20

DADDY KNOWS BEST

ALEXANDER ROBERTSON WEBSTER WAS BORN ON 29 JUNE 1926, in Kincardine, Scotland, a place as grey, cold and unforgiving as the soul it spawned.

He died 79 years later on 1 December 2005, alone at home, in the rather more salubrious surroundings of Braganza Court in Guildford, an upmarket private residential block.

In the intervening years, he had risen almost to the top of the ladder in his chosen police career, stymied in the end only by a commander's exam he could not pass, had become a senior freemason and was, in his dotage, kept busy as the president of his local Residents Association.

By 1946, Great Britain was shaking itself down after defeating Hitler and Sandy was a 20-year-old man looking for a future. He decided it was to be in the police service and moved south. He had failed the exam to join the Scottish forces, whose training centre, Tulliallan, was based just minutes up the road from his hometown.

By 1950, he had joined the Met and, as so often happens, become married to the job. It was the making of him, and it was the making of a marriage that would bring him two sons and a daughter.

He met former nurse Odette Blewett in the force, where they

worked together. On 19 December 1952, they married in East Horsley, Surrey, and settled down to life together in an austere Britain bankrupted by the war effort.

As we have seen, it was rather an odd household, and Odette lived in the shadow of her 'Victorian' husband throughout their marriage. Indeed, when she died of cancer in October 1997, only seven people turned up for her funeral, so withdrawn had she become from friends and extended family.

Sandy Webster, a tough disciplinarian, rose swiftly through the ranks, so much so that by the 1970s he was a detective chief superintendent in charge of the Fraud Squad at the Metropolitan Police Service, no mean feat.

By the early '90s, he had retired from the force, with a superb pension and a long-service medal.

He also took a keen interest in his son's affairs.

The question that remains with any investigator who looks at the evidence of Malcolm Webster's crimes is a simple one: how did he get away with it for so long?

Why wasn't he traced earlier? Stopped earlier? How could so many chances to stop his spree in its tracks have been missed by those in authority?

The answer to these questions may lie not with Webster, or with those who tried desperately to force Grampian Police to reopen the inquiry, but possibly with his now dead father.

It is a fact that he made telephone enquiries to Grampian Police in the early days after the horror crash in 1994 which killed Claire Webster. It is also a fact that he contacted the Foreign Office when his son ran into trouble in Abu Dhabi, over the unexplained deaths of three children. It was 'Daddy' – as Webster called him until the day he died – who arranged flights back to the UK, with the help of the Foreign Office. This has been confirmed by investigators close to the case.

In fact, bizarrely, no paperwork can be found now to show Webster was even there, although there are plenty of party pictures from his time with colleagues that place him in the country. They say he worked at Tawam Children's Hospital in the capital. Health chiefs there say they have no record of that.

One co-worker said, 'I remember him well, he was a creepy guy.'

What is the truth behind the allegation that Webster was responsible for the deaths of three children in a special ward at an Abu Dhabi hospital? That he was playing God with these young lives, experimenting with dosage levels of insulin.

Certainly, detectives in Aberdeen made inquiries, but the trail was too cold and, in the absence of the corpses for forensic examination, they soon hit a wall. The three children had all died in 1989, during a six-month spell where Webster worked at the hospital.

As with most high-profile stories that grip the attention of the public across the globe, tales began to emerge of Webster's past almost as soon as he was convicted.

Detectives at Grampian Police were reported to have investigated whether the Black Widower had been experimenting with dosage levels of drugs at the hospital ahead of killing first wife Claire and attempting to kill second wife Felicity.

Webster flew into a rage when he read of the allegation. He immediately contacted his solicitor, Aberdeen-based John McLeod of Mather & Co, and instructed him to issue a full denial. It was an unusual move for the man who kept his own counsel throughout the inquiry and who answered police questions with a firm 'no comment'.

Whether true or not, the news that he was even suspected of harming children was enough to provoke him into action. Webster vehemently denies any involvement in the deaths of the children and, met with a wall of silence from the Abu Dhabi authorities, it is difficult to establish whether he is, for once, telling the truth.

Certainly, his solicitor would appear to be in no doubt. John McLeod dismissed the allegations almost as soon as he heard of them. 'Not only does he deny them, he has never been formally accused of any of them. These issues are not new. They have been well ventilated in the two years it took to prepare the case. They have not got to the stage where an allegation has been made.

'To my certain knowledge, no investigation was even begun, let alone concluded. This story emerged based on the feelings of a former lover who had misgivings about the deaths of three children. It was, quite frankly, without foundation.'

The former lover who made the claims said she was shocked into action after reading about how Webster had drugged and killed his first wife, and attempted the same with his second.

She said, 'I was stunned and could not believe what I was reading. The three children went into cardiac arrest and subsequently died. It's not very common. He was the one who found them and raised the alarm.'

Attempts to elicit a truthful response or statement from Webster on this were also met with a wall of silence.

His solicitor John McLeod said, 'Malcolm is not talking to anyone ahead of the appeal. He has enough wood to avoid being in contact with the denizens of the press while there are matters outstanding. The charge runs to hundreds of pages. The appeal is ongoing. As far as I am aware, no investigation was started into Abu Dhabi, never mind concluded. Not only does he deny having anything to do with the deaths of children in Abu Dhabi, he has never been formally charged with any of this. As far as I can see, it's nonsense that has gone nowhere in terms of any inquiry.'

The Aberdeen Press and Journal, a Scottish paper that took a keen interest in the Webster case and whose reporters have close ties with Grampian Police, reported that officers 'were looking at whether the anti-epilepsy drug Clonazepam was involved in the deaths'.

It does seem strange that three children under the age of six can die in the same ward and be found by the same man.

However, the ward was an intensive-care ward and the man who found the little bodies was a nurse working there.

We know that Webster went on to become a cold, calculating killer. But his later crimes were for financial gain, and it would appear he had nothing to gain from killing these children.

These are questions only Malcolm Webster knows the answers to. Did he inject sick children and watch them die as he worked the night shift in an Abu Dhabi hospital? Certainly, no parent to date has come forward to demand an inquiry.

His father's role in this particular scandal is of more interest, as he was still working at the Met in London at the time, in charge of the Fraud Squad. Sources close to the case have told me that he placed calls to the Foreign Office at the time, requesting assistance to get his son out of the Saudi state.

Malcolm had called to tell him there was a problem, that some children had died, and he was being interviewed over the deaths.

That was enough for Alexander Webster, who decided that his son would be safer in London, while the Riyadh authorities conducted their probe, than sitting there waiting for an outcome. At least if it went badly, there would be an extradition process to go through. He would not be a sitting duck.

'Daddy' also funded the airline ticket home.

Some five years later, Webster drugged his first wife and killed her in a fake car crash.

Two years after that, he met New Zealander Felicity Drumm while they were both working in Saudi Arabia.

Had he been struck off or investigated in Abu Dhabi, would he have been able to obtain another medical role in the same region? By the time he met Felicity Drumm, he was working as a medical sales rep, not a nurse. She was working as a nurse in the capital city, Riyadh. Perhaps Webster, knowing he could never get back on to a ward, plumped for the next best thing.

The allegations surrounding the children's deaths were

examined ahead of Webster's trial, but there was insufficient evidence to proceed.

Alexander also smoothed Webster's return to the UK from New Zealand in 1999 as authorities over there were closing in on him. International arrest warrants were issued in New Zealand for Malcolm Webster. Nobody in the country acted on them, much to the consternation of the New Zealand detectives working the case.

Webster even tried to return to that country a short time after those warrants were issued and was refused entry at the airport. He was sent back to the UK via Australia, but not arrested on the spot. Officers have since said there was not enough evidence at that time to detain him. In reality, they didn't want him in the country in case he targeted Felicity and their son. From the moment she had gone to the police, they had placed a warning flag on his passport, so worried were they that he might try to sneak back to finish her off.

Alexander Webster died in 2005. It was only after his death that things started to move and officers from Grampian began looking again at the case.

That Claire Webster's tragic death was labelled an accident shook several senior members of the investigating teams who were there on the night. Police officers, unable to shake from their minds what they had witnessed at the scene, worked the case in their spare time. Firefighters with years of experience of car smashes also refused to believe Webster's version of events.

He lied at the scene to several witnesses, the car was loaded with accelerants and he had escaped the crash unscathed while his poor wife had been unable to flee. Why? At least two witnesses saw him on the grass verge before the car was aflame. What stopped Claire Morris from getting out of the vehicle? That question was eventually asked, but it took police almost 17 years to answer it and it led us to where we are today, with a danger to society safely locked up, where he should be.

From 1999, officers in New Zealand had been asking for

something to be done in the UK about Webster. Felicity and New Zealand detective Glenn Gray battled unsuccessfully for a decade to get Grampian to reopen the crash that killed Claire.

Some feel there may have been hidden angles to this case all along, although this has never been properly investigated and therefore cannot be officially endorsed. It's true to say, however, that Alexander Webster held a rank in the Met which is one below commander and two ranks below assistant commissioner, also that he was a hands-on cop, and sometimes brutal. He had retired at the time of the crash that killed Claire, but it's not outside the ranks of possibility that he might have tried to get involved.

Certainly there are suspicions that he might have placed telephone calls to Grampian police officers at the time of the car crash that killed his daughter-in-law. Did he ask to be kept informed about the progress of the inquiry, or make a point of labelling the crash a tragic accident and claim that his son was struggling to come to terms with it? As there are no records of such calls, we have to assume that Grampian officers would deny that they ever took place.

Felicity Drumm, who survived Webster's two attempts on her life, hated Alexander Webster. When Webster was finally convicted, she said, 'I only wish his dad was alive to see it.'

Alexander Webster had taken the time to issue chilling threats to Felicity. He told her she would never get custody of their son, that he would see to it that she was deemed mentally unstable.

He paid for Malcolm to fight for custody of young Edward through the New Zealand courts, at a time when he was well aware of arrest warrants in place for his son. At a time when he knew that his son was being investigated for trying to kill her, and for a series of arsons. He funded the court cases where Webster claimed Felicity was not a fit mother, hoping his investment would see his grandson brought back to the UK. He also funded Webster's flight back home to the United

Kingdom, when he knew that police in New Zealand wanted to talk to him.

A senior police source in New Zealand was troubled by Grampian's response to questions raised. He said, 'We could not understand how, despite repeated requests for help with the case, it kept being batted back. We knew how dangerous he was, and we made damn sure they knew how dangerous he was, yet nothing was done.

'Then the old man died in 2005 and a year later they're reviewing the case. It just struck us as very odd. The arrest warrants were international warrants; his father would have been aware of them.'

Although there is no hard evidence that Webster senior applied pressure to slow down the investigation, and there are other reasons for the apparent police procrastination, evidence was heard in court that there had been calls for an inquiry into why some decisions were made.

A traffic sergeant was told by a police officer in no uncertain terms that the case was being closed as an accident. The officer spoke of that being very unusual, as two of his own men had been voicing their concerns over the crash.

Grampian's handling of the case was also criticised by a senior Strathclyde detective, one of the men directly involved in the Simone Banarjee case. Former Strathclyde Detective Inspector Charles Henry said a series of missed opportunities allowed Webster to dodge justice from 1994 until his eventual arrest in 2009. He was so concerned he urged the force to launch a full internal inquiry into why they ignored repeated warnings about Webster.

Mr Henry said, 'Any woman who was in a relationship with Webster was at risk, especially if things were not going well for him financially.'

He added, somewhat diplomatically, that there had been 'missed opportunities' surrounding the death of Webster's first wife Claire in a fireball car crash. 'They had a forensic report which suggested it was accidental at that stage. There was also a lot of disquiet as Webster had told police there was no one in the car while his wife was getting burned alive. The failings at that time endangered the lives of at least two women in Oban and others whom he appeared to be grooming.'

Although praising the police work that took place after 2008, Claire's brother Peter Morris also voiced his concerns over the initial probe, going as far as to demand an apology from the men in charge of it. 'I have questions about why it took until 2007/08 for the case to be thoroughly investigated.'

Understandably, Peter is still very angry at some aspects of the case and with the way the original investigation was conducted, allowing Webster to go free for nearly two decades. He said, 'The fact of the matter is that, in 1994, a murder was not detected.'

He has called on those who made mistakes back then to have the honesty 'to apologise to my mother and myself', and added, 'I am not asking Grampian Police for an apology, I am asking the people who made mistakes to apologise. I understand that people have reputations to protect, but my sister lost her life and I feel that is more important.'

Detective Chief Inspector Phil Chapman, who led the reopened inquiry, said, 'Hindsight is a great thing. We were hugely challenged because of the complexity of what had happened.

'What was available to them back then . . . it's a different world. I know there has been some criticism but we had to employ cutting-edge techniques.'

There were concerns internally that there was corruption with Grampian Police in 1994. Their chief constable at that time, Ian Oliver, had set about drumming out corrupt officers from within its ranks.

The force, and particularly its undercover units and drugs squads, had been seriously compromised by organised-crime gangs. The extent of the corruption was so serious that outside forces had to be brought in to mount operations and at one point a Scottish Crime Squad operation against dealers in the city of Aberdeen was stood down when their target walked out of a building, looked up to the window where Crime Squad officers were positioned to surveil them, winked, waved and walked off. Someone had given the career criminal the heads-up.

Not only that, he was wearing a police-issue earpiece and had been instructed to listen for a particular noise he would hear if secure communications were being used around him. Only an insider could have provided such clear instructions and equipment.

It was because of incidents like these that Oliver took action and cleaned out a host of cops. Four years later, he took early retirement after a tabloid newspaper published details of his personal life and criticism was raised over his handling of a high-profile murder investigation. There were suspicions voiced at the time that Oliver sowed the seeds for his downfall in the force when he took on the campaign against internal corruption.

Claire Morris died in the crash orchestrated by Webster that same year. Both his parents were police officers, well schooled in detection. Could one of them have been capable of muddying the waters on their son's behalf?

For the sake of Claire's family, for the sake of Felicity, Simone and all those targeted, and for the integrity of the Grampian force, it is imperative that an independent inquiry is established into the events of that night and the failings surrounding it. A young woman died. At least three more could have. While there is no suggestion that officers who worked the case on the ground were in any way complicit, the victims believe an inquiry would help heal some old wounds.

21

A MAN OF LETTERS

MALCOLM WEBSTER HAS BEEN LABELLED A PSYCHOPATH, A sociopath and a black widower. A cad, a philanderer and a liar. He may be all these things, but he is also a father.

He would appear to be a dad who does not possess the same emotional responses as most people. Experts have argued over his exact classification, but we can perhaps glean a snapshot of the real Malcolm Webster from a series of letters he sent to his son and estranged wife Felicity Drumm.

In the letters to Edward, now 13 and building a new life with mum Felicity in New Zealand, we can get a glimpse of a man who would appear to care about something at least, his own flesh and blood.

He speaks of playing cricket, badly, and rugby, fishing and computer gaming.

He also sent his son a photo of himself when he was aged around 12. In his school uniform, Webster looks like any other young schoolboy of his era, a side parting and wonkily knotted tie. At the time he sent Edward the snap, he had shaved his head and was faking cancer, so could hardly have sent a more up-to-date photo.

Of course, once his son gets older and joins the pieces of his dad's life together, he will come to realise this deception

237

took place at the same time he received the cheery letter.

Is this natural behaviour for a sociopath? The experts tell us that this is behaviour Webster has learned from others around him, as he is incapable of expressing or feeling it for himself.

There is a poignancy in his writing, even though he types and prints them out on his computer rather than writing them out. However, he does start and end the letters in his own hand.

He signs off 'Love Daddy' and finds himself in the unenviable position of having to ask his own son Edward whether he prefers to be called Ned, as his mother Felicity has taken to calling him, or Edward.

How many fathers across the globe can relate to that? A marital split rends the lives of the children as well as the parents.

However, the underlying statement from Webster in this question to his son is that he does not care for Ned as a name and prefers Edward. This is a subtle challenge to Felicity's decision to rename her son, a break from the past, a small victory for her. Webster in his letter to his son attempts to redress that slight, in the psychological war of attrition that exists between the parents.

To prosecutors in the case, it seemed incredible that Webster could write letters to his son and speak of such things as angling at a time when he was faking cancer and, indeed, robbing the local angling club.

His arrogance allowed him to write the letter, so sure was he that his crimes, committed on different sides of the world, would never be joined together.

He had escaped unpunished thus far, who was to say that would ever change? And, 13 years later, he must have felt sure that his murder of Claire was now something nobody could successfully prove against him.

Webster does appear to have a genuine warmth for his only

child. When Felicity told him she was pregnant in 1997, his immediate reaction was one of anger, which quickly subsided into acceptance. Felicity was stunned by his reaction, but, unbeknown to her at that time, he was probably worried that the drugs he was slipping her in her tea and food would show up in blood tests at the maternity hospital.

She has always said that, after the fire set by Webster at her parents' home, he would have been a happy man had he been able to walk out of that house cradling baby Edward as she and her parents burned to death. It would have solved all his problems in one fell swoop.

Within the coldness of the man, there is some warmth, somewhere deep and hidden, for his son and heir. It may be that the joy of fatherhood competes with the psychotic tendencies of a man who cannot properly feel, or it may be that he wants his son to hear the story of his dad's life from his father, not from those around him who were directly affected by his actions.

Whatever his reasons, Malcolm Webster sat down to write seemingly anodyne letters to his son at a time when he knew the net was closing in. Were they part of a premeditated act by him to show his human side? Did he want to convince only his son, or the rest of us too, that he was actually a normal man whose life had been filled with misfortune?

He sent his son a typewritten letter and some photos, one of which shows him fishing, another shows the new country home he has just purchased.

> I have also been fishing quite a lot and as you can see from the photo I have been fortunate in catching some good fish this year. I was secretary and treasurer of the local club. I don't know if you have been fishing yet, but it's good fun.
>
> I also have a little boat and go out sea fishing sometimes when the weather is good. I normally catch mackerel, which are really nice to eat, and as mackerels go around in

large groups called 'schools' when you catch one, you catch dozens.

Describing the photo of himself holding a large fish, he continued:

> This is a rainbow fish, it was caught a few weeks ago. I have also moved house, and now live in the middle of the countryside, which is really lovely. It is very peaceful here and very safe, everyone knows everyone and there is no need to lock the car, apart from when one goes to the city.
>
> I plan on getting a couple of dogs at some stage, have you any idea as to what I should call them? I would be interested in your thoughts.
>
> It has always been a wish of mine to keep bees and because of the location of the house it should now be possible, although I need to go and learn how to look after bees before buying them!

A man guilty of stupefying the women in his life in order to kill them and steal their estates learning to keep bees, and chatting idly about the prospect of buying a couple of dogs. It is an idyll far removed from the reality of his situation at that time, when plain-clothed officers were following his every move and his third wife-to-be was being lined up for assassination.

His letter continued:

> So what else to tell you, well I have changed jobs and this has meant that I have been very busy. I cover a large area and therefore have a lot of driving to do. I have ordered a new car and will send you a photo when it arrives in November, that's of course if you are interested in cars; I certainly was when I was a boy.
>
> We have different cars over here than you do in New Zealand, but the new car is an Audi A3 2.0 Tdi sports

quattro if that means anything to you. What are your hobbies? I guess football, cricket and the PlayStation! Am I correct!

By this time Webster had sent his son a PlayStation 2 console, but had reneged on various promises to send pocket money. He was also pleading poverty to Simone Banarjee in Oban. In another letter, he wrote:

My Dear Edward, hope that this letter finds you really well and happy. I am sorry that I have not written back sooner, but it has been a very busy time over here and this has been the first time I have been able to really sit down and write you a letter, BUT rest assured you are in my thoughts all the time.

Now, I call you Edward as that was the name Mummy and I called you when you were born in Scotland, however, I know that Mummy calls you Ned, so you need to tell me what name you would prefer to be called, of course I could continue to call you Edward and Mummy call you Ned if you would like!

A quick question for you. Did you get the baseball bat, glove and ball that I sent you from the States in April? First of all, please find enclosed £100, please go and buy something nice with this. I am delighted to hear that you are enjoying the PlayStation 2.

Of course Christmas is not that far away so you will have to have a really good think as to what you would like from me. Talking about that PlayStation, there will be a new version PlayStation 3 coming out next year, and as I will be buying one for myself I will of course get you one.

As I said it has been a very busy time and I thought you might like to know what I am up to. Like you I have been playing cricket a bit this year, it was good fun and we won most of our games. I am a bit of an all-rounder and at the 'old' age of 46 I am not as fast as I was, however, all the other players I play with are my age so it's not too bad! I don't know if you saw the Ashes on the TV, it has been a very interesting time in the UK this summer, both teams were very close, and really either could have won at the end, lucky for me England won!

Anyway Edward, I had better get on, I will be in touch soon, and remember to get back to me on your Christmas present, the post takes longer at Christmas time, so the sooner you tell me the better.

Enjoy your money and have fun. Remember that I love you very much. Love Daddy.

Thought that you might like to see a photo of me when I was at school (many years ago . . . I think that I was about 12 when this was taken).

The stream of consciousness in this letter to his son speaks of lots of pastimes and activities but lacks any real warmth, except right at the end when he states, typewritten, 'Remember that I love you very much.' He then signs, with a flourish, 'Love Daddy'.

Felicity had allowed her son to write back to the father who she knew as a monster. It must have been one of the most difficult decisions of her life, but she has tried to be as open as possible with Ned when he asks about Webster.

Felicity says, 'My son is more aware now. I try to protect him but I'll always answer his questions. He knows his dad took all my money. He feels embarrassed about who his father is.

'I felt so humiliated at the breath-taking extent of his deception and how I was so immersed in it. The only thing that became reassuring to me was that everyone else had been equally convinced by him. Obviously, I wouldn't be here if it hadn't been for Dad. I'm incredibly lucky. He's a psychopath, and things, possessions and people are expendable if they meet his ultimate need.'

While Webster was writing letters of love to his son, discussing the cricket and angling, his letters to estranged wife Felicity adopted a rather different tone. He was matter of fact, cold and uncompromising. He told her lies about proceedings in Scotland in an effort to silence her claims that he tried to kill her and that he stole her money.

A stunned Felicity must have fought hard to suppress the urge to rip up the letters after first reading, but by that time she had turned detective against Webster, and knew at some point in the future his words to her would be important evidence. They were stored away.

At the time, warrants were in place in New Zealand for his arrest for stupefying and attempting to kill her and for a series of arson attacks at homes linked to the couple.

To say the letters are strained is an understatement, but they give a fascinating insight into the mind of a man who knew he was responsible for these acts but was able to construct a letter threatening legal action against his estranged wife for repeating them.

Interestingly, he also speaks of his father, who Felicity had argued was central to his son's ability to evade capture for so long.

Felicity,

I hope that this letter finds Edward happy and in the very best of health.

My solicitor has asked me to inform you, as a matter of courtesy, that papers were last week lodged with the court in Scotland to start divorce proceedings against you, and I am of course happy to do this.

In 1999 you and your father made wild and untrue allegations against me and for some bizarre reason Felicity, you even made allegations against my father. As you are only too aware, I was never allowed to defend myself against those allegations in New Zealand.

It should therefore come as no surprise that, whilst of course you are at liberty to make any statement to the court you wish, I have instructed my solicitor that should you or anyone else decide to make these allegations again, separate legal proceedings will be taken out against that person or persons. You can not go round making these allegations, unless you are prepared to prove them, they are simply untrue, and whilst this will result in a very considerable cost from both parties, it is something I am quite prepared to do.

There is no legal aid available in Scottish divorce proceedings.

On a separate and more cheerful note, I intend to start writing to Edward each month, he is now at an age where he should know more about his father and also know how much I miss and love him.

I also intend to start sending Edward monthly allowance/ pocket money. This is of course not maintenance, as you have stated many times in letters (copies held) that you would not accept maintenance for Edward from me.

It should be pointed out here Felicity that I will never understand why you would make such a statement (as others have wondered as well) as the only person that this affects is of course our son Edward. I have to tell you that I find it bizarre.

Bizarre is probably the correct word here. Incredible would be another. Felicity, in her reply, keeps matters straightforward, simply asking him to send any monies for Ned via her as the youngster did not at the time have his own bank account.

Felicity had opened one for him, but, when the promised payments from Webster failed to appear, she closed it down again. She refused to tell her son that Webster would be sending him money, although, when he did receive the trickle of gifts and small amounts of money, she made sure he knew who had sent them.

By the time he wrote this letter to Felicity, Webster was a worried man. It is evident that he was writing the letter to cover his back. The threat of divorce proceedings was a lie, and it would appear he is more upset at the allegations levelled at his father by Felicity than he is about the claims concerning his actions. He is wanted by the New Zealand Police at the time of writing, and twists this to suggest he has not had the opportunity to clear his name in court as the authorities would not allow him back into the country to do so.

In fact, they refused him entry to New Zealand because they feared he was returning to finish the job.

The letter is interesting for the lack of regret, remorse or any hint of apology within it. There is no acknowledgement of any responsibility on his part for the position in which they find themselves.

Then, it is as though he flicks a switch in his head and writes at the foot of the letter that he intends to communicate with his son, that he should know who his dad is. He even begins this paragraph with 'on a separate and more cheerful note . . .'.

It would appear that Malcolm Webster has, in his own mind, boxed his son away from the rest of the madness for which he is responsible. He cannot see the tragedy of including such a paragraph at the foot of such a cold, hard letter. His son, when he is old enough to understand all that has gone on, will see it in all its arrogant, ill-judged glory. Webster will certainly regret writing it, and probably already does, given that it featured in his trial as just one more example of the lies he spun across the globe.

While I was researching Webster for this book, I discovered that the Black Widower has written to various people from prison, mostly friends and family. Women, including some of the women who featured at his trial, have also put pen to paper to correspond with him once again.

I wrote to him at HMP Barlinnie to tell him I was writing this book. I offered him a chapter in this book to explain himself, perhaps to apologise. He did not respond, on the advice of his lawyer.

He has yet to write to his son, or Felicity, again, and he has yet to write anything, to anyone, resembling an apology.

22

PRISONER 111737

MALCOLM WEBSTER'S ENTIRE LIFE HAS NOW BEEN REDUCED to a number. That prison number is 111737.

When he was found guilty, he entered the behemoth that is the UK prison system and was given only his new numeric identity, along with the standard-issue prison uniform of trousers, sweatshirts, socks and pants.

And that was it. The sum total of a life of deceit and murder. It is hugely ironic that the Black Widower, who killed, drugged and burned so he could have the finer things in life, has ended up in prison with nothing. Not even the clothes on his back are his own.

He was moved from HMP Barlinnie to HMP Shotts, one of the country's toughest jails, a few weeks after he was found guilty and properly immersed in the prison system. Shotts Prison is a barren, soulless place in a town of the same ilk halfway between Edinburgh and Glasgow, a prison with a tough reputation where some of the country's hardest men are held. Career criminals.

He is in protective custody, which means he cannot be held alongside the men in the general population of the prison. He is a 'beast' to his fellow cons, someone they believe killed children and a coward who targeted women, drugging and killing or attempting to kill them.

The worst thing you can be in prison is a child killer. The second worst is someone who kills women.

Malcolm Webster, in the eyes of the cons around him, was both. He was, therefore, a marked man and spent much of his early custodial days isolated from the other inmates.

Imagine being so scared of those around you that you refuse to even shower. Webster retreated into himself and only spent time in the one area he knew was secure, his cell. He refused to wash and fellow cons complained to officers about the smell.

What a shock to Webster's system after a life of living high on the hog, with other people's money.

Many inmates doing time for killing will have acted while under the influence of drink, drugs or passion. This made Webster an even more likely candidate for a severe beating; he did it simply for money.

Whether he is guilty of the crimes against children in Abu Dhabi or not, it is enough in prison that the suspicion is there, when angry men have nothing else to do with their time except plot.

One got to him just days after he was transferred and unleashed hell on the Black Widower. The con's lightning-quick attack was over in a matter of seconds and left Webster with a badly broken nose, severe bruising to his eyes and a nasty gouge on the top of his head. The angry inmate had attacked him with a metal pole. He was lucky to escape with his life as the attack was quickly spotted and prison officers pounced to pull him to safety.

The shock to Webster's system, his psyche, must have been immense.

Now he cannot be placed back with those same men. It was a clear message to the governor: 'We do not want him in here.' The prison code had spoken. Any governor who does not listen at such times is liable to be dealing with a body and a murder inquiry at some point in the near future, hardly good press.

While inside Barlinnie jail, he paid a recently convicted

paedophile wrestler for protection. Jim Brown was paid by Webster to sit with him in his cell and to escort him to and from the gym and canteen. Brown was taking the Black Widower to the gym with him in an effort to toughen him up. Evidently, it hadn't worked.

The 24 year old also escorted his charge to the showers, so that Webster could finally wash after days of refusing to do so out of fear.

Brown, who was caught with a hoard of child porn at his home in Holytown, Lanarkshire, in Scotland, was also convicted of performing a sex act on himself in a swimming-pool cubicle in Wishaw.

The bronzed power lifter had 15 minutes of fame on TV when he appeared on ITV dating show *Take Me Out*, hosted by Paddy McGuinness. The Scotsman entertained viewers by whipping off his kilt to reveal a skin-tight wrestling outfit. But the woman he was sent on a date with branded him a control freak who stalked her after the show.

Webster's fledgling arrangement with Brown petered out when prison bosses told him he was being moved. HMP Barlinnie tends to be merely a holding jail for inmates recently convicted in the west of Scotland. They are immersed in the prison system there for a few weeks, before being sent elsewhere to serve the remainder of their sentences.

When news of Webster's arrival at HMP Shotts filtered through to inmates, they didn't like it. People like Webster, they thought, should be in HMP Peterhead, in the far north of Scotland, a jail that is unique within the prison system for being almost completely populated by sex offenders, rapists and child abusers.

The system seems to think that housing these men together under one roof minimises the chances of their being attacked, but even within their ranks there is a pecking order, and Webster, were he to be sent there, would only manage to come about halfway up it.

His life, wherever he goes, will be a living hell. Relatives of his victims may say 'at least he's living'.

Webster is effectively on suicide watch again inside HMP Shotts and his fellow inmates, now that they have sensed blood, will be relentless and ruthless in their pursuit of him.

Bosses at the jail are trying to ensure that he gets into some kind of daily routine, and are looking to give him a 'trusty' job where he would spend most of his time with the prison officers, away from the rest.

He is a cold, calculating killer, just like the other men inside that institution, but the difference is Webster did not learn his trade on the streets growing up. He is that rarest of killers, a genuine psychopath who killed to enrich his life with the trappings the kill gave him. The killers around him would have acted out of love or money. They will never understand him, and he will always be terrified of them. His crimes may have been of such despicable violence one can hardly appreciate the full sweep of them, but he never lifted a hand in anger physically to achieve his aims. The men around him do their talking with their fists.

Webster has also converted to Islam. This is partly because it affords an inmate more prayer time every day and also because the food is much better. It's a common ploy among inmates, who suddenly rediscover their heathen ways the minute they shake off their prison chains.

However, he had another reason to convert. He hoped the Muslims inside the jail would help protect him once he was one of them, a minority. He hoped they did not have the same strong feelings about men who abuse and kill women. He was wrong.

He has been roundly shunned by most of them. One other man, inside on drugs charges, agreed to be Webster's protection, for a fee. It didn't last long and the man backed out when he realised the strength of feeling about Webster's presence in the jail.

The people who do want to be his friends are the people Webster despises, those who prey on the young and the weak. Before long, he will have to come to terms with the fact that he is one of them.

The attack on him at Shotts has left him weak and vulnerable. He has withdrawn into himself, according to sources, and is causing prison doctors and senior staff a headache. He is a difficult man to fit into the system, a square peg in a round hole.

I wrote to Webster and offered him a chapter in this book, a place to explain his actions and, if he so desired, apologise for them. He has yet to write back. At the time of writing, there is another book being written about him and a New Zealand TV company has signed up some of his victims for a dramatisation of his life and crimes.

He has said very little throughout. At the very beginning, when the story first broke, he sent me a series of emails in which he denied all charges against him.

> When all this is over and the police are satisfied I had nothing to do with any of this, I'll give you an exclusive. It's nonsense. I know you are only doing your job, and I am happy to co-operate with the police. I'm not hiding from anyone. The truth will out.

He complained to the Press Complaints Commission in 2008 after news of his crimes first appeared in the *Sunday Mail* newspaper. He told the commission the article was 'a pack of lies' and added that his privacy had been invaded.

He also complained to Grampian Police after they shared information with their New Zealand counterparts, as both forces tried to join up the dots of his crimes.

On the advice of his lawyer, he now has nothing to say. Not until after his appeal is heard. Webster is getting plenty of mail though, and from some surprising people.

Women, lots of women, are writing to him at HMP Shotts. Some of the women who gave evidence at his trial have been in touch with him, as well as family members and old friends. They say he is suicidal.

Peter Morris, Claire's brother, has little time for such talk. He is busy trying to establish a foundation in honour of his sister, as a way of protecting the victims of crime, and continuing his fight to reclaim his sister's grave from Webster's control.

'I will also keep fighting as far as my sister's grave is concerned. I did not ask for this battle, but I will fight tooth and nail for what is right and proper.'

The investigation into Webster has not ended. Grampian Police and prosecutors believe there are other victims. Police in Australia and New Zealand are also keen to fill in some blanks in the killer's life story. There are gaps in the timeline. Police officers do not like gaps.

Webster went walkabout in Australia on at least two occasions and remained secretive about what he was up to for those periods in his life. According to Derek Ogg, the leopard does not change its spots, so there is a possibility that at some point in his life he has killed and not been brought to justice for it.

The trial and news of his arrest went quickly round the globe. The fact that nobody else came forward during his trial suggests detectives are looking for bodies, rather than witnesses.

There is a novel, written by Iain Banks, that Webster may want to look out in the prison library, if indeed he has not yet read it. Some feel he must have, so closely does the plot mirror his crimes. The novel, *The Crow Road*, is set in rural Scotland, and has been made into an acclaimed BBC drama.

The similarities are quite remarkable. The novel tells the story of a man who drugs and kills his wife in a staged car crash on a rural Scottish road but is discovered and prosecuted some years after the event.

The most striking thing about *The Crow Road* is that it was published in 1992, and reached its peak sales at the same time Malcolm Webster murdered his first wife Claire, in exactly the same manner.

It could be just the kind of misinformation Webster rails against, like the Abu Dhabi 'lies' he feels got him beaten up in prison.

Webster's charge sheet at his trial was a lengthy one. It ran to 11 full pages and detailed the extent of his crimes spanning a 17-year period. He cannot really and truly claim that he is the victim of a smear campaign.

As we have seen in an earlier chapter, the 'rap sheet' contained the more obvious allegations of capital crimes against the middle-class monster but also included some lesser charges necessary to prosecute the case on Scottish soil.

In early spring 2012, Malcolm Webster was granted leave to appeal his conviction. The grounds for that appeal are not yet known but, given what his solicitor John McLeod has already confirmed, he will try to beat the guilty rap by claiming the jury was misdirected in some way. The amount of paperwork involved in the appeal is vast.

Webster is claiming he suffered a miscarriage of justice and that the punishment part of his life sentence, 30 years, was 'excessive'. Mr McLeod has even said that his client has been treated worse than the Lockerbie bomber. He said the jail term was longer than that handed to Abdelbaset al-Megrahi, the man convicted of the Lockerbie bombing, who received a 27-year term.

Webster's appeal will argue that the jury in the case was misdirected by the judge, Lord Bannatyne.

Mr McLeod said, 'The grounds of the appeal against both conviction and sentence are complex. Some relate to a misdirection or an absence of direction from the judge. If this was a murder, then it is a terrible thing. But we believe 30 years was an excessive sentence; it is more than the Lockerbie bomber received.

'I can't say too much about what the grounds are. Malcolm will not be talking to anyone until after it is heard and decided.'

However, what is clear is that, once again, Webster refuses to accept his guilt.

Derek Ogg QC does not think much of his chances: 'Doomed to fail,' was all he would say.

In the meantime, it is expected that Webster will eventually be housed at HMP Peterhead, where all of the country's serial sex offenders end up. If they are all in the same boat, there is no need for segregation, or so the theory goes.

There, no doubt Webster will learn from others around him. He will be taught where he went wrong, how he should have done it, how to make it more foolproof. The only saving grace is that, barring a successful appeal against his conviction, he will never again be free to perfect his crimes in reality, on the outside.

He will be 82 before he is eligible for parole. He might make it, although his victims may be hoping he dies in jail long before that day ever comes around.

TIMELINE

18 APRIL 1959:
Malcolm John Webster and twin sister Caroline are born in London to Alexander, a police officer, and Odette, a former nurse and police officer.

The young Malcolm is an isolated child, given to lying and fire-raising.

1974:
Malcolm leaves school at 15 with no formal qualifications; he is involved in petty crime but there are no records of any police or social services involvement.

1976:
After a short career in sales and as a binman, at 17 Malcolm decides to train as a nurse.

1978:
Coming to the end of his nursing training, he gets work in a nursing home and starts a relationship with the 15-year-old daughter of the owner. He is sacked for stealing from the home. His girlfriend becomes pregnant and has an abortion.

He ends the relationship soon after.

He begins another relationship, his first true love. Few details are known, but, after it ends, she commits suicide.

He falls in love again, this time with a married woman who has separated from her husband. After a few months, she returns to her husband, leaving Webster devastated.

CIRCA 1980 TO 1990:
Webster goes travelling around New Zealand, Australia and to the Middle East over a decade-long period.

He leaves his nursing job at Tawam Children's Hospital in Abu Dhabi after an investigation into the unexplained deaths of three children in his care, and returns to the UK to take up a nursing job in Guildford, Surrey.

1991:
Malcolm meets Moorfields Hospital nurse Claire Morris at a party. They begin a relationship, and move to Aberdeen where they both work for Grampian NHS. Claire begins to study for a health care science degree at the university.

Family and friends can see she is truly, madly, deeply in love but mum Betty has reservations about her daughter's 'strange' new boyfriend.

3 SEPTEMBER 1993:
Malcolm and Claire marry in a traditional ceremony at Aberdeen's King's College Chapel. They move into their first home together, Easter Cattie Cottage near Oldmeldrum, Aberdeenshire. Claire complains of feeling constantly tired, but attributes it to the move north.

SPRING 1994:
Claire Morris tells her mother, Betty, that she and her husband have been involved in a road accident, when their car ended up in a ditch, although neither of them was injured. She also

speaks of being constantly tired and visits her GP, Dr Francis Howarth, who notes she is 'fatigued'.

27/28 MAY 1994:

Webster and Claire set off from home at 11.30 p.m. to deliver a document to Aberdeen Children's Hospital in time for next morning. They crash on the Oldmeldrum to Auchenhuive road in rural Aberdeenshire, a back road and well off Webster's fastest route. Their Daihatsu 4X4 leaves the road, crashes into a tree and apparently catches fire. Webster tells police he jumped from the driver's side, saw trees blocking the passenger door and tried to pull Claire across the seats and out through the driver's door, before collapsing and losing consciousness. When people arrive to help, Webster tells them there is nobody in the car.

Claire Morris dies in the fire eight months after marrying Webster. She is just 32.

Despite misgivings from Claire's friends and family, as well as witnesses who attended the scene, a Grampian Police investigation concludes Claire's death is a tragic accident.

Senior officers within Grampian Police tell traffic sergeant David Allan that 'a line had to be drawn under' the investigation.

Webster spends seven days in ward 50 of Aberdeen Royal Infirmary, from where he organises Claire's funeral.

Less than a week later, Webster has cashed in the insurance policies on Claire's life worth £208,000.

7 JUNE 1994:

Webster attends Claire's funeral in a neck brace, and appears inconsolable. He is supported by Claire's family.

By this time, Webster has bought a new car and is in the process of buying himself a yacht. He has relationships with a number of women in the months following Claire's death, including with Geraldine Oakley, who is working in the hospital where tissue samples from Claire's body are stored.

NOVEMBER 1994:
Webster has spent most of the £208,000 insurance payout.

DECEMBER 1994:
Webster lands a job with an IT company selling specialist medical computer software to hospitals in Saudi Arabia. He leaves Scotland for the Gulf state.

MAY 1996:
Webster meets New Zealander Felicity Drumm, a cancer nurse, at a leaving do for mutual friends in Riyadh. They fall in love and Felicity says Webster is keen to move the relationship along. Felicity tells Webster she has earned enough working in the Gulf state to be living mortgage-free with NZ$98,000 in savings.

JANUARY 1997:
Webster proposes to Felicity on holiday. A delighted Felicity accepts.

26 APRIL 1997:
Webster marries Felicity at St Andrew's Church in Auckland. They honeymoon on Cooks Beach, on the Coromandel Peninsula. She falls asleep on the first night of their honeymoon after drinking a cup of tea and doesn't wake up for 36 hours. Webster is unfazed by her concern at this, and says she 'must have needed it'.

MAY 1997:
They decide to relocate to Scotland after Webster gets a job in Aberdeen. A routine blood test shows a problem with Felicity's liver. Symptoms displayed mirror those for victims of date-rape drugs.

SEPTEMBER 1997:

Felicity discovers she is pregnant with their son, Edward. Despite being initially angry, Webster starts to look forward to the birth.

Webster sets fire to furniture at their home in Lyne of Skene. Felicity arrives home to find him at the property telling her he got there 'in the nick of time'. He is unharmed, but files another insurance claim. Felicity loses vital identity documents in the fire.

MAY 1998:

The couple's son Edward Drumm Webster is born. They decide to return to New Zealand.

12 NOVEMBER 1998:

In anticipation of their move to New Zealand, the couple have placed all of their belongings in storage at Shore Porters Society, Aberdeen. The storage facility burns down on the same day that Webster visits to retrieve some paperwork. The blaze destroys £5 million in antiques, paintings and valued possessions, and the Websters lose everything. There are delays with their insurance claim and Webster refuses to leave Scotland until it is settled. Webster finally gets a £68,000 payout from insurers.

LATE NOVEMBER 1998:

The family returns to Auckland and moves in with Felicity's parents. Felicity puts a NZ$60,000 deposit on a house in Takapuna, while Webster says he is having trouble transferring money from Scotland.

There is an arson attack on the Takapuna house.

10 FEBRUARY 1999:

Webster deliberately sets fire to an armchair at Felicity's parents while everyone is asleep, endangering the life of his wife and nine-month-old son Edward and Felicity's parents.

12 FEBRUARY 1999:

On the way to sign the paperwork on the new house, Webster and Felicity have a crash. They are unhurt, but Webster feigns a heart attack to stop Felicity going to the bank to sign papers for their new house.

18 FEBRUARY 1999:

A drugged Felicity is woken in the car at a picnic spot by a call from her father Brian who has discovered Webster has systematically emptied her bank account, and he insists she comes home. Webster denies any wrongdoing. Felicity finds insurance policies bearing her forged signature and she is found to have a strong sedative in her system. She believes Webster intended to kill her as she slept.

As Felicity tells all to police, Webster heads for the airport and a flight back to the United Kingdom, via Australia.

He later fails to appear in court on a number of charges. International border alerts for Webster are issued.

19 AUGUST 1999:

Webster attempts to enter New Zealand, but is refused entry.

2000:

Arrest warrants are issued for Webster. He faces four charges, two fire-raisings, attempted murder of his wife and the stupefying of Felicity with drugs.

2002 TO 2005:

Webster is in a relationship with Christina Willis. At his suggestion, they make out wills and power of attorney forms in each other's favour.

5 AUGUST 2004:

NHS theatre manager Simone Banarjee meets Malcolm Webster at a hospital in Oban, Argyll, where they are both working. Webster discovers she is independently wealthy with a trust fund. Webster ends his current relationship.

DECEMBER 2005:
Simone and Webster begin a relationship. Webster's father dies, and on the day of his funeral Webster phones Simone claiming he has terminal cancer. After pretending to undergo chemotherapy, he shaves his hair to continue the deception. He is having relationships with at least three other women.

JANUARY 2006:
Concerned for Webster's health as she believes he is undergoing cancer treatment, Simone invites him to move in with her.

FEBRUARY 2006:
Simone changes her will, leaving her estate to Webster. Webster stands to gain more than £300,000 in the event of Simone's death.

SEPTEMBER 2006:
Webster proposes to Simone and gives her a £6,000 engagement ring.

2006:
On a work assignment in Leeds, Jane Drumm talks to a senior police officer about her sister's experience with Webster, putting in motion a new inquiry. Jane is interviewed by Scottish police officers.

JANUARY 2008:
Simone Banarjee is handed an Osman letter by worried detectives. It warns her that her life is in danger and details Webster's past. It also states that he is still married to Felicity Drumm and has a child with her in New Zealand. Simone says it seems 'all so unbelievable'. She initially refuses to believe what she is being told.

4 FEBRUARY 2008:

After Simone confronts Webster with the information police have given her, he walks into Aberdeen Royal Infirmary A&E claiming to be suicidal.

28 MARCH 2008:

Grampian Police announce they are reinvestigating the crash 14 years earlier that claimed the life of Webster's first wife Claire. They appeal for information about the 'dry run' before the fatal collision.

30 MARCH 2008:

My exclusive story reveals Malcolm Webster is being hunted by police over a crash involving Felicity. Webster is by now somewhere in the UK and has been spotted in Oban as well as Devon and Cornwall. He surrenders himself at a police station and is interviewed. He answers 'no comment' to all questions. He is released without charge but must report to police daily.

DECEMBER 2008:

Ann Hancock, who has been seeing Webster since 2007, is handed an Osman letter.

2 FEBRUARY 2009:

Webster appears in private at Aberdeen Sheriff Court charged with murdering his wife in Aberdeenshire 15 years earlier, as part of a life insurance fraud.

10 FEBRUARY 2009:

Webster appears in court again, this time also charged in connection with his second wife.

1 FEBRUARY 2011:

Webster's trial begins at the High Court in Glasgow. He is charged with murdering Claire, attempting to murder Felicity and intending to bigamously marry Simone Banarjee to gain access to her estate, along with a series of fires and frauds. The charge sheet runs to 11 pages. He denies all charges against him. The longest trial of a single accused in the history of the Scottish legal system gets under way, with witnesses from across the globe, both in person and via video link.

3 MAY 2011:
The prosecution case closes after 50 days of evidence. The jury have heard the women in his life speak of druggings, lies, deception and premeditated murder. A steady stream of women arrive at court to tell their stories of love and betrayal. Webster is exposed as a serial philanderer.

5 MAY 2011:
Malcolm Webster takes the stand at the High Court to give his account of events. He denies murdering his first wife and attempting to murder his second, and says his first wife's death was an accident. He tells the court, 'I did not kill my wife.'

12 MAY 2011:
Jury hears closing speech from the Crown. Webster is a 'brilliant criminal genius' who got away with murder – and that his fatal flaw was 'he can't stop himself'. If convicted, Webster would become one of the most notorious modern-day criminals, the jury is told. Advocate depute Derek Ogg QC says in his closing speech that the accused is 'a most cruel, practised deceiver'.

19 MAY 2011:
It takes jurors less than four hours to find Malcolm John Webster guilty.

THE BLACK WIDOWER

5 JULY 2011:

Webster is caged for 30 years and is told he is a danger to women. Barring a successful appeal of his conviction, Webster will be 82 before he is eligible for parole.

CONCLUSION

HOW DO YOU CONCLUDE A CASE LIKE MALCOLM WEBSTER'S?
You cannot. It is still ongoing.

There are investigations still running in the UK, Australia and New Zealand, all linked to what Malcolm Webster was eventually convicted of.

His path of destruction has left some splintered lives, perhaps some not yet found.

However, we can try to take some findings from it, learn from it, in an effort to prevent it happening again.

There were so many warning signs. From an early age, should someone have questioned why this boy's nickname was Pyro? Had he received the attention from social services or the police back then, right at the start, could our societal checks and balances have changed the course of his life?

Did his middle-class upbringing and police officer father preclude this from happening? Possibly.

In the early days of Webster's criminal career, in the weeks after he had killed Claire Morris, could Dr James Grieve have run his office with a lighter touch, thus encouraging his staff member to actually knock on his door and voice her concerns about her new boyfriend Malcolm, who was asking strange questions about the death of his first wife and probing her as to where the tissue samples were stored?

Dr Grieve was by no means an ogre, and is not only a consummate professional but also a thoroughly decent man, but something stopped her from taking him into her confidence and, had she done so, this case could have been wrapped up in 1994 as a murder. Grieve himself has been left pondering this question, as so many others have. They all still carry the shadow of the time Malcolm Webster walked through their lives.

The downside to the scenario of Webster being caged back in 1994, of course, is that, by now, he might have been back on the streets, having served his time, young enough to prowl once more.

It is truly a fascinating case, one of the few where the perpetrator maintains his silence and, by doing so, leaves us with more questions than answers.

It is evident there were some glaring errors in the initial investigation into Claire's death, both at the scene and in terms of Webster's background. He was in huge debt at the time of her death, a fact apparently completely missed by the original inquiry team. He had crashed off road a month before. Her mum Betty Morris told police this when they came to tell her Claire was dead.

At least four emergency service personnel voiced concern at the incident being labelled an accident, and that's without counting the list of friends and family who were concerned at the time.

They were told to forget it and move on. Had their voices been heard, and some inquiry undertaken, other victims might not have had to endure such suffering at Webster's hands.

Why didn't doctors pick up on the tell-tale signs of doping in his female victims? The signs were plain to see. Why did Grampian Police refuse to reopen the case between 1999 and 2007, despite repeated requests by New Zealand Police to do so? There was an inter-jurisdictional failing here, something senior officers admit but now claim has been fixed. Inter-agency police work is improving as the world gets smaller, thanks in large part to the technology available today. Cops no longer need to fly to the other side of the world, they can now Skype.

In terms of his fire-raising, why weren't insurance companies sharing information on this serial claimant throughout the 1990s? They do now, but that is a relatively recent procedure that did not happen in 1994, except within insurance circles within the same town or city. He claimed for a dead wife, a house fire and for the fire at Shore Porters, between 1994 and 1999. All of the claims originated within Aberdeenshire, but that was not red-flagged. Had questions been asked at the time of the fires, could it have led police to look again at his young wife's death five years earlier?

The only people who can truly hold their heads high in this case are the victims, the officers of the New Zealand Police, the new Grampian Police investigation team and those who raised concerns only to see them batted away.

By the time Malcolm Webster arrived in Oban, and set fires both at his friend's house and at the local hospital where he worked, alarm bells should surely have sounded. Add to that a stolen laptop from the hospital, which involved police charges, and the embezzlement of thousands from the local angling club, and we are left wondering how, in a town the size of Oban, could all of this go unchecked and be so badly investigated?

When he shaved his head, plenty of people in the west coast town refused to believe his cancer story and hit the nail on the head when they said he was hiding behind it to avoid facing up to his crimes.

Some were quoted in the press saying just that when the stories of his life began to break. The angling-club member, who took over as treasurer, perhaps deliberately, said he always thought there was something 'fishy' about Webster. But then he had been suave enough to talk his way into that position of responsibility in the first place.

There are 8,500 permanent residents of Oban. They have a decent-sized police office there, as the town is the casting-off point for policing the islands around the west coast, most of which remain unmanned or have only a single officer based there.

A man arrives in town, gets a job at the hospital, is linked to two fires, steals a laptop, steals from the angling club, and then claims to have cancer. A quick check by any cop would have thrown up the fireball crash back in 1994 that claimed the life of his young wife.

Hindsight may be 20/20 vision, but surely mistakes were made in terms of ending Webster's reign of terror there and then? Unfortunately, it was already too late for most, and the probe into his affairs had begun.

Going back over the evidence we now have to hand is always much easier than finding it at the time, and from the moment the new inquiry properly got going in 2006/07 it was faultless.

Also faultless was the manner in which it was prosecuted. Lord Bannatyne took time to thank both sides at the conclusion of proceedings, remarking it was as good a case to showcase the Scottish justice system at work as any.

He also excused the jury members from ever having to be called to do their duty again. After the gruesome sights they had seen, and the length of time they had committed to the case, they would have been thankful for that.

As were the victims, all of them. The family and friends of Claire Morris, Felicity and her family, Simone and hers. All those other women sprung from his clutches. They all now share a common bond, one that will stay with them forever, touched as they were by the life choices of a man who still believes he is innocent, and cannot understand why he is in jail, among the lowlife.

Of everyone connected to the case, of all the victims, the

cops, the prosecutors, the witnesses, the jury members, the solicitors, there is one voice that has not been heard, and that is as it should be.

Somewhere in New Zealand, a 13 year old boy is, no doubt, playing games on his PlayStation, going to school and chatting with his friends on Facebook, using a shortform textspeak language alien to anyone over the age of 25.

He loves rugby, cricket, music and his mum, probably in that order, although hopefully that ranking will rearrange itself as he grows older. He has already had to live with the taunts from the school bullies, put them out of his head and get on with his schoolwork. The people who really matter in his life would never say such things.

That boy will never know his father. His mother knew him, and regrets everything except the 13 year old she gets up for school each morning. Even when he grows older, and perhaps begins to resemble the man she first fell in love with, the man who turned into such a monster, she will remain resolutely in love with the only thing Malcolm Webster ever gave her. A son.

Edward Drumm will no doubt grow up, become curious and read about his missing father's crimes. He will be both incensed and horrified.

Perhaps, of all his victims, Malcolm Webster, has done him the greatest damage.

In September 2011, Peter Morris embarked on a walk from his sister's graveside to the Scottish parliament building in Edinburgh, a distance of some 150 miles, in an effort to raise funding and awareness for a new foundation to be set up in Claire's memory. He hopes to call it CLAIRE – standing for Caring Loving And Invigorating Retreat Environment.

Despite having to go to hospital for four days halfway through the gruelling walk, and sadly losing his right leg below the knee, Peter, 48, eventually managed to deliver a 6,000-name petition to ministers calling for the foundation to be established. His campaign garnered support from the likes of comedian Billy Connolly.

At the time of writing, it was being discussed by Scottish ministers with a view to funding a £1 million retreat centre for victims of crime, an incredible achievement.

It's too late for Claire Morris and her family, but they still hope and pray the retreat centre will happen, for the sake of others. What an achievement it will be, for a family riven by such terror, to create something so lasting for others. The ministers who saw Peter at Parliament were struck immediately by his humility and modesty, in the wake of all that had happened. They were so impressed he might just have talked them into parting with a sizeable chunk of money at a time when every penny in the treasury is being guarded fiercely. But he had right on his side, and it is testament to him and his family that they took their experiences of death and turned them into a positive for others.

'I have gone through the feeling of guilt and thought, "Why were we not suspicious enough?" We might have been able to save Claire if we had done or said something.'

He feels that question will live with him forever. Malcolm Webster will live in the minds of plenty of people, long after those who followed the court case have forgotten him as he languishes in prison. All the victims, all the people he hurt, the people he robbed and walked away from without so much as a backward glance.

And he is still hurting people. If it hadn't been for his killing spree, Peter Morris would still have his sister, his lower right leg and his peace of mind. The sentence he has been left with is wondering if he could have done more.

The words of the man who put Webster in jail for life sum him up more eloquently than anyone else could. Derek Ogg said, 'Malcolm Webster is a brilliant criminal genius with one flaw: he couldn't stop himself.'

ENDNOTE

AT THE TIME OF WRITING, MALCOLM WEBSTER WAS GRANTED leave to appeal the severity of his sentence. An appeal against conviction was dismissed, then re-submitted, and he was also granted leave to appeal his conviction in March 2012.

The decision in Scotland sparked utter outrage from the families most closely connected to his crimes.

His lawyer John McLeod said his client would be making no comment on the appeal process and added that it could be well into the latter part of 2012 before any outcome could be expected.

The appeal centres on the defence submission that the jury was misdirected and that the length of his sentence, 30 years, was excessive.

Claire Morris's brother Peter reacted angrily to the news, urging Scots judges not to lower his tariff. 'I feel it is outrageous that they have allowed him to appeal his sentence. Do the Scottish public want a man like this in their midst in less than 30 years?' he said.

'He is very evil, very conniving, and for them to spend even more money on him is outrageous. I wonder how much of the Scottish taxpayers' money they are willing to spend on this man.

'It feels like, for me, I'm in a personal battle wi..
and I will not stop until he has confessed his crimes. H.
not confessed to anything, but I will keep endeavouring to
make sure that he does so.'

Webster's defence in court, on legal aid, cost the taxpayer
more than £300,000.

Webster's lawyer, John McLeod, confirmed a second bid to
appeal the conviction. His appeal to reduce the sentence has
already been granted. That should be heard in the coming
months.

Mr McLeod added, 'I am not able to discuss the details of
the grounds, but there are eight separate grounds of appeal
against conviction, and two separate grounds of appeal against
sentence.'

Malcolm John Webster, a cold and calculating killer, is the
only man in the world who believes he has been unjustly
convicted.